# FUTURE PROOF

# PROOF

## THE GREATEST GADGETS AND GIZMOS EVER IMAGINED

C000145247

NICK SAGAN WITH ANDY WALKER

AND MARK FRARY

Copyright © 2007 Elwin Street Limited

Conceived and produced by
Elwin Street Limited
144 Liverpool Road
London N1 1LA
United Kingdom
www.elwinstreet.com

Published in the UK in 2008 by
Icon Books Ltd, The Old Dairy
Brook Road, Thriplow
Cambridge SG8 7RG
email: info@iconbooks.co.uk
www.iconbooks.co.uk

Sold in the UK and Ireland
by Faber & Faber Ltd, 3 Queen Square
London WC1N 3AU or their agents

Distributed in the UK and Ireland
by TBS Ltd, TBS Distribution Centre, Colchester Road
Frating Green, Colchester CO7 7DW

ISBN: 978-1-84831-004-9

No part of this book may be reproduced in any form, or by any
means, without prior permission in writing from the publisher.

Design and artwork by Sharanjit Dhol
Original illustrations by Richard Burgess
Additional text by Sam Hiyate

Images reproduced by kind permission of the following:

Abiomed: page 62; Big Stock Photo: page 54; Corbis: pages 75, 81, 91;
Dreamstime: pages 21, 24, 34, 50, 56, 64, 71, 72, 87, 114, 118, 121,
132, 154; iStockphoto: pages 83, 95, 104, 112, 126, 137, 139, 140,
142, 150, 156; The Kobal Collection: pages 12, 19, 38, 85, 76, 98, 128;
NASA: pages 22, 23, 26, 37; Rex features: pages 11, 41, 68; Science
Photo Library: pages 76, 103, 106; Seiko: page 88; Shutterstock: pages
92, 101, 116, 125, 130, 144, 149; The Stanford Racing Team: page 42;
Transition: page 14 (images courtesy of Transition Inc. and Benjamin
Schweighart); The United States Navy: page 49; Urban Aeronautics:
page 8 (Image copyright © 2006, Urban Aeronautics Ltd.)

Printed in China

# FUTURE PROOF

## THE GREATEST GADGETS AND GIZMOS EVER IMAGINED

NICK SAGAN WITH ANDY WALKER

AND MARK FRARY

ICON BOOKS

# CONTENTS

## 1.00    TRAVEL AND TRANSPORTATION    8

## 2.00    COMPUTERS, CYBORGS AND ROBOTS    38

## 3.00    COMMUNICATIONS    68

# INTRODUCTION ∴

∴ So you wake up ready for the big presentation with all the facts and figures already stored in your head, having absorbed them while you slept using hypnopaedia. Your alarm clock greets you by name, tells you the news and weather, and asks what you want for breakfast so the automated kitchen can get started. You shower and dress and can't find your lucky left sock, but fortunately all your clothes are smartlinked, so your lucky right sock can tell you where its twin is hiding. That sorted, there's time for a quick bite to eat, dished up by your helper robot, followed by the daily supplements that radically extend your lifespan. You step outside, locking your door and activating your home security system merely by visualising an image – it could be the colour of your lover's eyes, an oak leaf, or the hamster you had when you were six – in a biometric passthought keyed to your unique brainwave pattern. And then it's off to the office – but wait, which vehicle will you take? The jetpack? Or the flying car?

Doesn't sound like your day? Not mine either. And yet it's the sort of lifestyle we've heard about for decades. Tex Avery's *House of Tomorrow*, *Car of Tomorrow* and *TV of Tomorrow* cartoons; Walt Disney's 'living blueprint of our future', Tomorrowland; Hanna-Barbera's fundamentally optimistic (if bureaucratic) contribution, *The Jetsons*: these fantasies of what is yet to come serve only to tantalise us, seeming like they should be possible today but remaining ever out of reach. It's almost enough to make one think there's a conspiracy afoot.

In science and science fiction alike, recent years have seen much talk of 'Singularity' – a hypothetical boom in our development where we find ways to boost our natural intelligence and then pop out world-changing technologies at an astonishing rate. Perhaps we can be forgiven for thinking that we're a long way away from this exciting new stage in human evolution when we can't even manage to pop out inventions we hyped half a century ago.

So where are these broken promises, these technofigments? Where is our Moon colony? Our worker droids? Bionic limbs? Force fields? You'd think that wonders such as these would be commonplace here in this new millennium, a time that once appeared so impossibly far away. Instead, they're conspicuously absent, like guests of honour who've yet to show up for their awards. Are they simply late to the party or have they got hopelessly lost? Should we cross them off the list altogether?

And what about the darker side of sci-fi: what if it's the dystopian visions that eventually come true, rather than the utopian ideal? Despite much doom-mongering about the dangers of future technologies, I think we're pretty safe. As my father, astronomer Carl Sagan, pointed out, 'Advances in medicine and agriculture have saved vastly more lives than have been lost in all the wars in history.' And thankfully, that drive to improve our human condition remains an essential part of our humanity. It cannot and will not stop. Every second of every day, our best and brightest work tirelessly to make tomorrow better than today. If we can do that – if we make each successive day even a little bit better than the one that came before – then we might just achieve the promise of the future.

So, what you hold in your hands is more than a book; it's an expedition in search of the future so many of us expected to see – and perhaps still might. As the legendary science fiction writer and inventor of the telecommunications satellite Arthur C Clarke once wrote, 'If we have learned one thing from the history of invention and discovery, it is that, in the long run – and often in the short one – the most daring prophecies seem laughably conservative.'

Nick Sagan, New York, 2007

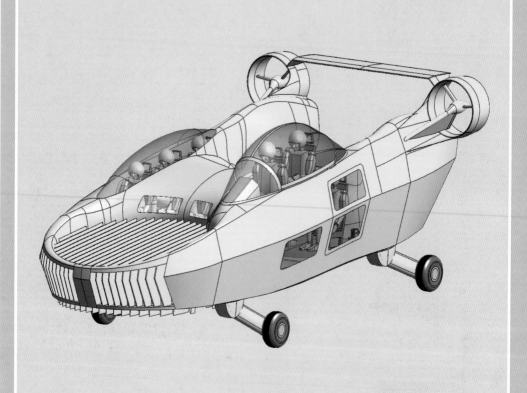

# TRAVEL AND TRANSPORTATION ⋰

'Where do you want to go today?' may have been a popular advertising slogan in the 1990s, but the year 2000 saw IBM summing up the frustrations of millions with an advertisement that asked, 'Where are the flying cars? I was promised flying cars. I don't see any flying cars. Why?'

It's an excellent question. Where are the jetpacks, the flying cars, the transporters and all the other advances that were meant to save us from the drudgery of our daily commute? Trapped in a line of slow-moving traffic, how can we not dream of alternatives? And how many man hours are lost in transit? How much extra pollution does road congestion kick up into the air we breathe?

While the potential for better means of travel has been evident for decades, jetpacks and flying cars symbolise the gap between our imagination and our ability to impose that imagination upon our world. And what about journeying beyond our world? Will our children and grandchildren holiday on other planets? Are the stars in fact our destination? And what about time travel?

So, let's put aside 'Where do you want to go today?' and instead take a good look at 'How are you going to get there?'

◀ The Civil X-Hawk, a rotorless vertical take-off and landing vehicle.

# JETPACK ⠸

*Imagine strapping on a piece of jet-powered luggage and, with the twitch of a joystick, being able to fly anywhere you like. No wonder the jetpack is one of the most popular icons of sci-fi: besides the joyriding thrill of travelling on demand in three dimensions, its practical implications would change cities into urban skyscapes whose inhabitants could conduct their lives off the ground, in a tier-to-tier existence unbounded by gravity.*

## ⠸ SCIENTIFIC HISTORY

Military organisations around the world have long seen the potential of the jetpack: the US military funded research by an engineer named Wendell Moore in the 1940s, and the Germans developed basic jetpack technology during the Second World War by strapping two pulse jet tubes of low thrust onto the body of a pilot. This device, known as the *Himmelstürmer*, was intended for use by German pioneers to cross minefields and bridgeless waters.

More recently, a company called Trek Aerospace has begun developing their own version with military and industrial uses in mind. However, the past 60 or 70 years haven't seen any substantial improvements in performance. Bell's original 'rocket belt' used hydrogen peroxide gas as fuel and could propel its pilot into the air for about 20 seconds. By the 1960s he had only increased flight time by 10 seconds.

The limited fuel capacity of a jetpack remains a barrier to its development even today. Millennium Jet's 2000 SoloTrek XFV – powered by a dual rotor, making it more of a personal helicopter than a jetpack – can hover only a few feet off the ground and suffered several accidents in testing. Trek Aerospace's Springtail EFV-4B uses a similar dual-rotor design that has improved stability and

| 1940s_ |
| --- |
| Bell Aircraft Co designs a rocket belt; flight time 20 seconds |

control but can fly for no more than 30 seconds. Still, the potential uses of the jetpack – personal and commercial as well as military and industrial – encourage scientists to continue to work towards a viable prototype.

## ⸬ REALITY

⸬ The major problem with the jetpack is its limited flight time. All of the examples mentioned here use hydrogen peroxide as a propellant. When combined with a silver catalyst, hydrogen peroxide decomposes into a mixture of superheated steam and oxygen. The hot steam and gas mixture is led into one or more jet nozzles to produce a reaction mass, creating the acceleration that enables the jetpack to take off.

▲ The 1991 incarnation of Rocketeer.

The great advantage of hydrogen peroxide is that, while the exhaust is very hot, it is still much cooler than that produced by combustion fuels, reducing the risk of fire or injury. However, the problem with hydrogen peroxide is that it's simply not possible to carry enough fuel to fly for more than 30 seconds, with a maximum range of 244 metres (800 feet).

Add to this the potential mayhem of hundreds of jetpack-borne people hurtling through the skies at any one time, and it's easy to see why jetpacks are, for the moment, relegated to spectator events and won't be available at your local shop any time soon.

The introduction of the jetpack outside fiction was the result of

**1984_**

Bell's jetpack appears at the Los Angeles Olympics

**1965_**

Bell's jetpack appears in the movie *Thunderball*

## ⸬ SIGHTINGS IN SCI-FI

- Buck Rogers first popularised the jetpack in his 1920s comic strip. In the 1930s *Rocketeer* comics and the subsequent 1991 film, the plot is all about the jetpack – with good guys and bad guys fighting to get their hands on the prototype.

- In the 1960s, the animated *Jonny Quest* featured a jetpack-clad hero. And in Japan, *Astro Boy* showed the popularity of the jetpack across the globe.

- James Bond ignited a new flurry of interest in the jetpack by using one in *Thunderball* (1965); as the

be-suited spy straps himself in, he quips, 'No well-dressed man should be without one.'

- In *Return of the Jedi* (1983), bounty hunter Boba Fett's jetpack works against him as Han Solo accidentally activates it, propelling Fett into the waiting maw of the monster Sarlacc.

- Steven Spielberg's 2002 film *Minority Report* sees the crime-prevention units of the Precrime Department using jetpacks as standard means of transport.

two high-profile flights, the first in the 1965 James Bond film *Thunderball*, and the second at the opening ceremony of the 1984 Olympic Games in Los Angeles.

*Thunderball* actually involved two jetpacks. One was a non-functional prop worn by Sean Connery (playing Bond), while the second was a genuine Bell Rocket Belt. Bell company pilots Bill Suitor and Gordon Yaeger performed the actual flying scenes.

The second famous appearance of the jetpack in public was at the opening ceremony of the Los Angeles Summer Olympic Games in 1984. Bill Suitor flew above the heads of spectators, many of whom instinctively covered their heads with their hands. The flight was seen by 100,000 spectators at the ceremony and watched on an estimated 2.5 billion televisions around the world.

▲ Sean Connery as James Bond (with jetpack) in *Thunderball*.

The future of the jetpack looks bright. NASA and the US-based Federal Aviation Administration (FAA) are working on a new air-traffic control system that will eliminate the need for control towers and ground-based radar systems at small airports, so greater use of personal aircraft should be possible in the coming decades. But perhaps the most promising future for the jetpack lies in a powerpack that doesn't rely on chemical combustion. In 2006, UK-based scientist Roger Shawyer reported the development of a tiny engine with no moving parts that generates thrust without emitting exhaust. This thrust comes from trapped microwaves bouncing back and forth along the length of a hollow tube with closed ends. The tapered nature of the tube allows the bouncing microwaves to exert more pressure at one end than the other, creating thrust. Shawyer hopes his 'emdrive', as he calls it, will first be used by an aerospace company to power a spacecraft. Meanwhile, he is working on scaling the emdrive for use on Earth, in hovering cars and wingless aircraft. Perhaps, even, for jetpacks.

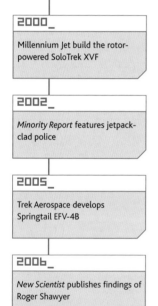

**2000**
Millennium Jet build the rotor-powered SoloTrek XVF

**2002**
*Minority Report* features jetpack-clad police

**2005**
Trek Aerospace develops Springtail EFV-4B

**2006**
*New Scientist* publishes findings of Roger Shawyer

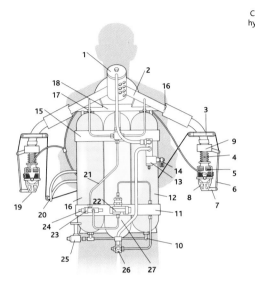

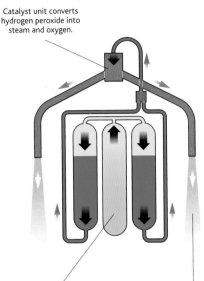

Catalyst unit converts hydrogen peroxide into steam and oxygen.

| 1 | Catalyst bed | 10 | Pressure valve | 19 | Rocket nozzle |
|---|---|---|---|---|---|
| 2 | Pressure pipe | 11 | Tank sling | 20 | Release control |
| 3 | Control pin | 12 | Fuel tank | 21 | Fuel pipe |
| 4 | Direction nozzle | 13 | Fuel pressure | 22 | Control guard |
| 5 | Fuel line | | gauge | 23 | Vents |
| 6 | Gear | 14 | Muffler | 24 | Cylinder gauge |
| 7 | Exhaust release | 15 | Tank sling | 25 | Safety valve |
| 8 | Converter | 16 | Fuel tank | 26 | Propellant |
| 9 | Convection | 17 | Feeder pipe | | pressure gauge |
| | nozzle | 18 | Control arm | 27 | Propellant tank |

Two cylinders of hydrogen peroxide pressurised by a cylinder of compressed nitrogen give about 25 seconds of flight.

Jets of high-pressure steam and oxygen provide around 140 kilograms (300 pounds) of thrust.

- Modern jetpacks remain close to Bell's 1940s design. Two canisters mounted on the pilot's back are filled with purified hydrogen peroxide. The pilot's controls allow pressurised nitrogen to push the propellant into a chamber, where it makes contact with a silver or copper catalyst.

- Hydrogen peroxide ($H_2O_2$) decomposes naturally to form water ($H_2O$) and oxygen ($O_2$) in an exothermic (heat-producing) reaction.

- Introducing a catalyst like silver or copper speeds up the reaction, resulting in superheated steam and oxygen at a temperature of about 743°C (1370°F).

- This gas mixture creates 140 kilograms (300 pounds) of thrust as it blasts out of the nozzles at the base of the jetpack. The pilot controls the direction of the exhaust to steer, and regulates the flow of exhaust to climb or descend.

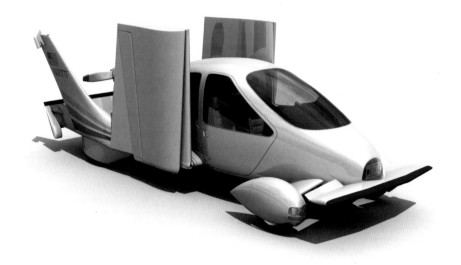

# FLYING CAR ⁞

*A vehicle that travels both on land and in the air means the choice is yours – drive to the shops for milk, or take off from your driveway and onto an automated skyway. The ability to commute in three dimensions at jet speeds would allow humans to live much further away from cities, reducing urban densities and improving land use.*

## ⁚ SCIENTIFIC HISTORY

⁚ More than 70 flying car patents have been filed with the US Patent Office since the beginning of the 20th century, but none has been mass-produced and only a handful have ever been built. Even fewer have flown and only two – the Airphibian and the Aerocar – have been certified as both road- and air-worthy.

Early flying car designs included the Curtiss Autoplane, which achieved a few short hops in 1917, and the 1937 Aerobile, made of many standard Studebaker automobile parts, which had some success but was shelved in 1957. Then there was the saucer-shaped Avrocar, a 'flying jeep' designed by the Canadian and British military to carry troops, which was abandoned in 1961.

The first prototype to be approved by the US Federal Aviation Administration was the Airphibian, designed by Robert Fulton Jr in the 1940s. The hybrid could fly at air speeds of up to 177 kilometres per hour (110 miles per hour ) and travel at half that speed on the ground. Its builders achieved more than 6,000 car-to-plane conversions. However, the most successful design to date has been the Aerocar, a fixed-wing plane-car hybrid. When in car mode, the wings and tail section can be removed and towed. In the air, the Aerocar has a range of 800 kilometres (500 miles) and a cruising speed of 217 kilometres per hour (135 miles per hour). It first flew in 1949 but a business deal to mass-produce the car went sour in the 1960s, killing any hope of commercialisation.

◀ The Transition car/aeroplane, courtesy of Transition Inc. and Benjamin Schweighart.

## Timeline

**1917_**
The Curtiss Autoplane achieves a few short hops

**1937_**
The Aerobile has some success

**1945_**
First prototype of Robert Fulton Jr's Airphibian

**1949_**
First flight of Mort Taylor's Aerocar

**1961_**
Canadian and British military design Avrocar

**1960s_**
Deal to mass-produce Aerocar falls through

▲ The Aerobile on display in the National Air and Space Museum, Washington, DC

## ⸭ REALITY

⸭ There are several promising flying car projects in development today. The Moller M400 Skycar is a vertical take-off and landing (VTOL) craft that inventor Paul Moller says will be available to buy in the 2000s in limited quantities. More than 100 people have paid a deposit for access to the first units, priced at US$500,000.

Moller's company has also started to produce the M200G, a small flying saucer capable of carrying two passengers, built to take off and land vertically. Designed as a low altitude all-terrain vehicle, it cruises 3 metres (10 feet) above the ground and can speed over difficult terrain such as swampland or rocky stream beds at speeds of up to 80 kilometres per hour (50 miles per hour ). Moller will initially build six, at a selling price of about US$90,000 each.

## ⸭ SIGHTINGS IN SCI-FI

- The flying car has become a staple in science fiction, ever since George Jetson's Spacion Wagon in the 1960s.

- Flying cars have also played a part in *Star Wars* (1977), *Blade Runner* (1982), *The Fifth Element* (1997) and *The Matrix* (1999).

- In *Back to the Future Part II* (1989), the DeLorean undergoes 'hover conversion' on a trip to the year 2015, rendering it air-worthy.

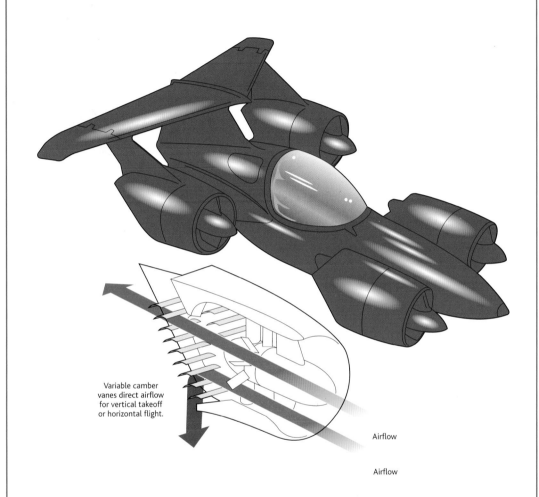

Variable camber
vanes direct airflow
for vertical takeoff
or horizontal flight.

Airflow

Airflow

- The most likely design for flying cars is a configuration called a VTOL, or vertical take-off and landing, aircraft.

- One example, the Skycar, is equipped with eight bucket-sized engines, two in each lifting pod. Each can pivot 45 degrees, and shutters inside the pod can pivot an additional 45 degrees to direct air flow so that the vehicle can switch from a vertical take-off configuration to forward flight.

- There are two parachutes that deploy if the aircraft suffers a serious problem.

# TELEPORTATION AND TRANSPORTERS ⁖

*Transporters that can get you from place to place without having to pass through the intervening space have fascinated scientists and sci-fi writers for decades. Imagine: no more traffic jams, commuting or transcontinental flights – and an easy way to extricate yourself from awkward social events!*

## ⁖ SCIENTIFIC HISTORY

⁖ Scientists have had some success in teleportation but are a long way from being able to transport anything larger than an atom, let alone a human. The first (qualified) success came in 1993, when a research team at IBM led by Charles Bennet confirmed that quantum teleportation is possible but only if the original object or person is destroyed. This problem has not yet been resolved. In 2004,

## ⁖ SIGHTINGS IN SCI-FI

- The word teleportation was first coined by American writer Charles Fort in his 1931 book *Lo!*, and since then the transporter has been ubiquitous in sci-fi under a variety of names, including the Vibra-Transmitter, Displacement Booths or Stepping Discs.

- The scientist in the 1958 film *The Fly* (remade in 1986 and 2006) experiments with teleportation, but accidentally includes a fly in his transportation with horrific consequences.

- Luckily for the characters of *Star Trek*, their transporter was a lot less risky. More recently, the 1994 film and subsequent TV series *Stargate* (with spin-offs like *Stargate Atlantis*) is based entirely on the premise of travelling to distant worlds through teleportation.

- However, bear in mind Douglas Adams' description of teleportation in his *Hitchhiker's Guide to the Galaxy* series: 'not quite as fun as a good solid kick to the head.'

scientists managed to teleport the quantum states of atoms but the original atom was irreparably affected in the process. However, scientists working on teleporting photons (particles of light) have had more positive results. In 2002, researchers at the Australian National University successfully teleported photons from a laser beam without affecting the original particle.

## › REALITY

› Scientists have found a way to teleport the properties of both photons and atoms using a quantum mechanics phenomenon called 'quantum entanglement'. Two atoms, A and B, are entangled. They then separate. A then entangles with a third atom, C, inheriting all of its properties but destroying it in the process. B continues on its way and entangles with a fourth atom, D, which then inherits the exact properties of C. While atom C is destroyed, atom D becomes an exact replica, even though no contact has been made between C and D. The problem is that scientists have so far succeeded only in transmitting the *properties* of photons and atoms, and the photon or atom being teleported is destroyed in the process.

Even if this process could be perfected, applying it to larger objects brings its own problems. The human body contains something like ten octillion ($10^{28}$) atoms. A massive quantity of data (estimated at $10^{22}$ GB) would have to be transmitted, stored and interpreted to reconstruct a human body after teleportation.

▲ The *Star Trek* transporter was 'the safest way to travel' in the 24th century.

## › TECH SPEC: QUANTUM ENTANGLEMENT

- While teleporting a person or inanimate object is currently impossible, the possibilities of quantum entanglement are being explored by scientists.

- In 2004, two teams of scientists, one in the US and one in Austria, teleported the quantum states of atoms and photons.

- If a functional teleporter were invented, the person or object being transported wouldn't be physically moved from one place to another. The process would work more like a computer scanner. An original would be scanned to record the precise quantum state of every particle in its body. This data would be transmitted to the teleporter's destination where each particle would be reconstructed in the exact same state to re-form the teleported body.

- The next part of teleportation technology is the hard part. The original would be destroyed. It's one thing to use a ham sandwich, but the cloning and destruction of your mum might be a little harder to accept. And is the exact copy at the other end still your mum or is it a clone? Scientists may one day make teleportation possible but the philosophers will have to figure out if it's an acceptable practice.

# 01:04_

# WARP DRIVES AND ANTIMATTER ENGINES ‹

*We have broken the sound barrier but we can't yet exceed the speed of light. If we ever want to venture beyond our own solar system, warp drives powered by antimatter engines may be the answer, as theoretically they provide ways of travelling faster than light.*

## › SCIENTIFIC HISTORY

› The major problem with faster-than-light travel is generating sufficient energy on board a craft to accelerate its mass. Scientific research has concentrated on antimatter as a potential source of this energy. Antimatter – the existence of which has been theorised since the 1920s – is a substance with physical properties opposite to matter. When it encounters matter, both are annihilated with a huge release of energy. Antimatter occurs naturally in high-energy

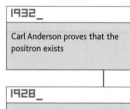

**1932_**

Carl Anderson proves that the positron exists

**1928_**

Paul Dirac suggests existence of antimatter

## › SIGHTINGS IN SCI-FI

- Sci-fi writers needed to invent faster-than-light or warp drives so that their space explorers could reach distant worlds in their own lifetimes.

- By the 1950s hyperspace travel was well established, starting with Isaac Asimov's *Foundation* and *Robot* series, which used hyperships with hyperdrives.

- In the bestselling *Dune* novels in the 1960s, Frank Herbert described moving at warp speed as

folding space, which semi-human Guild Navigators could accomplish thanks to the mystical effects of the spice-drug 'melange'.

- Today, travelling by warp speed has been rendered a cliché by *Star Trek*. *Star Trek* also popularised the idea that an engine fuelled by mixing matter with antimatter could be used to power a mammoth interstellar spaceship.

environments but isolating it for use as a fuel has proven difficult. Tiny particles of antimatter were first synthesised in 1995 at the CERN laboratories in Switzerland.

## ⫶ REALITY

⫶ An antimatter reaction is perhaps the most powerful energy source known to man: instead of tons of chemical fuel, only 10 milligrams of antimatter would be needed to propel a manned mission from Earth to Mars, and the mission would take only 45 days, as opposed to the 180 days projected for a craft powered by nuclear engines.

On the flip side, however, antimatter is not particularly common on Earth. Manufacturing antimatter in particle accelerators in physics laboratories is expensive: the 10 milligrams needed to fuel a Mars mission would cost about US$250 million. Meanwhile, the antimatter/matter reaction produces deadly radioactive gamma rays, which would lethally irradiate any passengers long before they reached their destination.

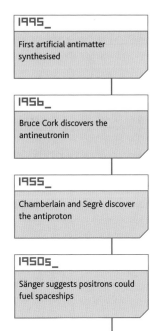

**1995_**
First artificial antimatter synthesised

**1956_**
Bruce Cork discovers the antineutronin

**1955_**
Chamberlain and Segrè discover the antiproton

**1950s_**
Sänger suggests positrons could fuel spaceships

## ⫶ TECH SPEC: POSITRON ENGINE

- Matter is made of atoms, which are in turn made of particles, including electrons, protons and neutrons.

- Reversing the charge on these particles creates antiparticles, mirror images of the originals.

- This 'antimatter' can then be used as an energy source by combining it with matter. When matter and antimatter come into contact they annihilate each other, producing enormous amounts of energy.

- The quantity of energy can be calculated according to Einstein's equation $E=mc^2$. The energy released (E) is equal to the mass annihilated (m) multiplied by the speed of light (c) squared. The speed of light is a very large number, so a huge amount of energy can be produced by a very small mass.

- The NASA Institute for Advanced Concepts (NIAC) is currently funding research into the possibility of using this energy as fuel. Their proposed positron-powered rocket engine would work as follows:

- Positrons are directed from a magnetic storage unit into an attenuating matrix (mixing bowl) that contains matter.

- The fuels react, releasing energy.

- This energy heats liquid hydrogen in the matrix, converting it to gas, which flows out of a nozzle. This produces thrust, which propels the ship.

- Warp drives – which work by changing the shape of the space around a ship so that distant points are brought close together – are considered mathematically possible but a viable mechanism for their operation has yet to be invented.

# SPACESHIPS AND SHUTTLES ⦂

*Ever since 1957, when the USSR launched* Sputnik, *the first man-made object to orbit the Earth, mankind has had a love affair with the spaceship. We've walked on the Moon, and have Mars and beyond in our sights. Whether we're exploring new solar systems on a starship or commuting from space stations to Earth on a shuttle, spaceships seem likely to have an important role in our future.*

## ⦂ SCIENTIFIC HISTORY

⦂ Russian Yuri Gagarin was the first man in space in 1961, aboard the rocket *Vostok*. In 1969, Americans Neil Armstrong and Buzz Aldrin were the first men on the Moon, aboard *Apollo 11*. Both missions used one-shot rocket systems to launch crew modules into space. The expense of these systems led NASA to pursue a reusable launch module and in 1981 *Columbia*, the world's first multi-use space vehicle, made its maiden flight and successful landing.

## ⦂ SIGHTINGS IN SCI-FI

- The spaceship has been popular in fiction since the Rocketship in Jules Verne's classic 1865 novel *From the Earth to the Moon*.

- Iconic sci-fi spaceships include the USS *Enterprise* from *Star Trek*, the eponymous *Battlestar Galactica* and *Star Wars' Millennium Falcon*.

- Interestingly, many of these spacecraft seem to be adaptations of seafaring vessels, right down to the use of archaic terms like 'fore' and 'aft' in describing movement in their starships.

- The *X-Files* and *Taken* use the Roswell sightings of UFOs as the basis for designs.

Shuttles allowed regular trips into orbit, launching satellites and building and supplying space stations, and recent years have brought robotic explorations of Mars and the construction of the International Space Station in orbit. However, these successes have come at a price: in 1986, the shuttle *Challenger* exploded 73 seconds after launch, killing all on board, and *Columbia* disintegrated on its return to Earth from orbit in 2003, with the loss of all seven crew.

## REALITY

*Ares I* and *Ares V* are the centre-pieces of NASA's Constellation Program for space exploration and space colonisation. They are intended to establish a moonbase and send a manned mission to Mars, after the shuttle programme is phased out in 2010. The smaller *Ares I* will transport astronauts into space and its heavyweight cousin, *Ares V*, will launch larger cargo payloads.

Emanating 1960s-era chic, *Ares* is the spacecraft NASA chief Michael Griffin once described as '*Apollo* on steroids'. The spaceship's conical capsule shape allows for the integration of an escape mechanism, which has become a priority after the shuttle disasters of 1986 and 2003.

▲ NASA's *Ares* craft are likely to be the next stage in space travel.

## TECH SPEC: NASA SPACE SHUTTLE

- Rockets overcome gravity by applying thrust, burning chemical fuel inside their fuselage. The burning creates exhaust, which is pushed downwards through nozzles. In keeping with Newton's third law (every action has an equal and opposite reaction), the exhaust pushes the rocket upward. When enough force is exerted, the force overcomes gravity and the rocket begins to climb upward away from the ground.

- At the launch of a shuttle, two solid rocket boosters burn solid fuel, which is made of mostly ammonium perchlorate (70 per cent) and aluminium (16 per cent). It is ignited and burns for about 2 minutes, generating 1.5 million kilograms (3.3 million pounds) of thrust – 71 per cent of the thrust needed for lift-off. The remaining thrust is generated by the three engines on the shuttle itself, which draw liquid fuel from the external fuel tank.

- Each engine produces 170,000 – 213,000 kilograms (375,000 – 470,000 pounds) of thrust. Once the solid rocket boosters have burned out, they are jettisoned at an altitude of 45 kilometres (28 miles) and parachute into the ocean for recovery and reuse.

- At 8.5 minutes into the flight, the shuttle engines shut down. The external fuel tank separates from the shuttle at 9 minutes and burns up in the atmosphere.

- At 10.5 minutes, the orbital manoeuvring system engines fire to put the shuttle into low orbit. Then, 45 minutes into the flight those engines fire again, putting the shuttle into a higher orbit, ready for its mission.

# SPACE TOURISM ⸫

*We're no longer content with exotic holiday spots on Earth, as the idea of taking trips into space for fun and relaxation grows in popularity. Who could resist playing in zero gravity, luxuriating at a Moon resort, or perhaps checking into an orbiting hotel? The more ambitious astrotourist could travel to Jupiter and ski Europa – the possibilities seem endless.*

## ⸬ SCIENTIFIC HISTORY

⸬ Since the 1950s, visionaries such as Barron Hilton, president of Hilton hotels, have dreamed of the possibility of space tourism. The world's first non-professional astronaut, Christa McAuliffe, met a tragic end as part of the crew of the 1986 space shuttle *Challenger*, which exploded shortly after lift-off, killing everyone on board.

However, the year 2001 saw the first space tourist, Californian businessman Dennis Tito, blast off in a Soyuz rocket from Baikonur, Kazakhstan, on a 10-day space mission that included a visit to the International Space Station. The prohibitive cost means this is unlikely to be a commonplace holiday choice any time soon: for his ticket and cosmonaut training, Tito paid US$20 million.

> **1986_**
>
> Christa McAuliffe joins crew of *Challenger*

◀ Bottom side up: the underside of a space shuttle.

## ⸬ SIGHTINGS IN SCI-FI

- It is no surprise that the first target for space tourism was our closest neighbour, the Moon: Robert Heinlein's *The Menace from Earth* (1957) tells the story of 15-year-old Holly Jones going on a flying holiday in Moon craters.

- Even earlier, Jules Verne wrote about Moon visits in *From the Earth to the Moon* (1865), and in Arthur C Clarke's 1961 *A Fall of Moondust*, we see that in the 21st century the Moon has been colonised and is open to tourists.

- Roald Dahl's *Charlie and the Great Glass Elevator* (1967) has Charlie and Willy Wonka docking at a Space Hotel.

**2006_**

Bigelow Aerospace launches
*Genesis I*

**2004-05_**

Branson and Rutan form The
Spaceship Company

**2003_**

Space Adventures obtains seats on
Soyuz missions

**2001_**

First space tourist, Dennis Tito,
takes off

◀ Astronauts on NASA
mission STS-098,
an experience that
might become a
reality for tourists.

In 1996, the Ansari X Prize Foundation offered US$10 million to the first non-governmental organisation to launch a reusable manned space vehicle to an altitude of 100 kilometres (62.14 miles) twice in two weeks. And in 2004, hotelier Robert Bigelow announced America's Space Prize: US$50 million for the first private American initiative to launch a five-person orbital space vehicle that can dock with his company's orbiting habitat. The Ansari X Prize was won in 2001 by Burt Rutan's company, Scaled Composites, with the craft SpaceShipOne, which is widely expected to be the future of space tourism. Virgin Group chairman Richard Branson has ordered five spaceliners from Rutan for his Virgin Galactic enterprise, which he claims will take paying passengers to sub-orbit by 2008.

## ⫶ REALITY

⫶ If you have US$200,000, you can already book one of 50 seats with Virgin Galactic to lift off from Virgin Earth Base. In a Gulfstream-jet-sized SpaceShipTwo, you'll take a two-hour flight to the edge of space to experience five minutes of zero gravity. Branson promises orbit and Moon flights next.

Several other companies – including PlanetSpace, Space Adventures and Rocketplane Limited – say they will compete to provide space tourism opportunities. Space Adventures has already put three private citizens into space, and also offers gravity-free flights on the Russian IL-76, dubbed the 'Vomit Comet', and on MiG jets flying to an altitude of 24,384 metres (80,000 feet).

# TECH SPEC: SPACESHIPTWO

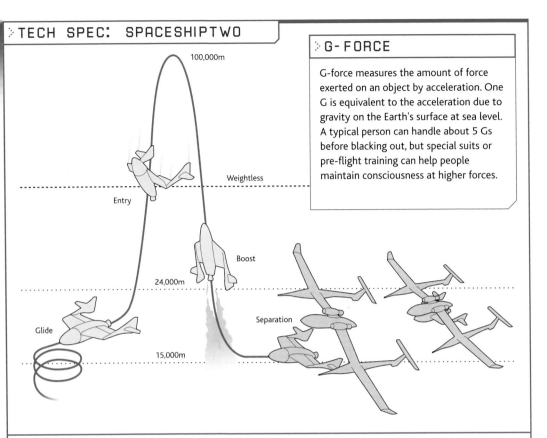

## G-FORCE

G-force measures the amount of force exerted on an object by acceleration. One G is equivalent to the acceleration due to gravity on the Earth's surface at sea level. A typical person can handle about 5 Gs before blacking out, but special suits or pre-flight training can help people maintain consciousness at higher forces.

- SpaceShipTwo – the improved version of SpaceShipOne – takes passengers into sub-orbit, allowing them to experience zero gravity.
- SpaceShipTwo is attached to a lifting mothership, which takes off from a runway and flies to an altitude of about 15,240 metres (50,000 feet).
- The spaceship separates from the mothership, glides for about 10 seconds, then ignites its hybrid engine. The engine contains hydroxy-terminated polybutadiene (HTPB), a common ingredient in rubber tyres. Liquid nitrous oxide (laughing gas) flows from a tank to the rubber fuel, where it accelerates the burn.
- The ship accelerates at 4 Gs and the pilot pulls the ship into a vertical climb. The engine burns for a full minute, pushing the craft to a speed of 3,200 kilometres per hour (2,000 miles per hour ).

- The engine burns out at 45,720 metres (150,000 feet), and the vehicle travels another 45,720 metres (150,000 feet) before it reaches the top of its climb. This takes four to five minutes, during which passengers experience weightlessness (zero gravity) and get dramatic views of the Earth and into space.
- To return to Earth, the pilot turns the ship so that it falls like a badminton shuttlecock, bellyflopping back into the increasingly dense gases of the Earth's atmosphere. Passengers experience 5 or 6 Gs, but with their pre-flight training they should be able to maintain consciousness. At 15,240 – 18,288 metres (50,000 – 60,000 feet) the pilot starts to fly the craft like a glider. It takes another 10 to 15 minutes to glide back to the airport where it lands like a conventional aircraft.

# TERRAFORMING ⋖

*As the future of our planet looks increasingly precarious because of global warming and overpopulation, the idea of colonising a nearby planet looks more and more appealing. Scientists think Mars has great real-estate opportunities, with its Earth-like proximity to the Sun and relatively easy access by spaceship.*

## ⋗ SCIENTIFIC HISTORY

⋗ In 1961, astronomer and astrophysicist Carl Sagan wrote an article in the journal *Science*, proposing the engineering of Venus for human habitation. While Saturn's moon, Titan, and Jupiter's moon, Europa, have also been considered since then, it is Mars that has become the planet of choice for terraformation. A 1976 NASA study of what it calls 'planetary ecosynthesis' concluded that there are no known obstacles to engineering Mars to become habitable. Sagan himself was to become an advocate for Mars terraformation, a position he defended until his death in 1996.

## ⋗ SIGHTINGS IN SCI-FI

- The word 'terraforming' was introduced by Jack Williamson in 1941 in a story called *Collision Orbit*, although the concept had been around since the 1930s.

- It became popular in *Star Trek II: The Wrath of Khan* (1982), in which the Genesis device that terraformed a dead planet also somehow brought Spock back from the dead.

- The 1990 film *Total Recall*, based on a 1966 novel by Philip K Dick, and the television series *Futurama* both present a future where Earth is overpopulated and a terraformed Mars is the new neighbourhood.

- In 2002 the TV series *Firefly* showed what terraformed planets and colonies might look like in the 27th century.

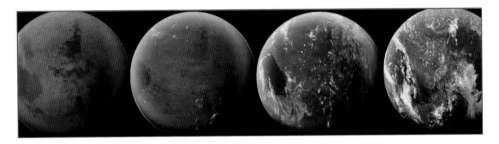

## ⟩ REALITY

⟩ Although getting the raw materials to Mars to begin terraforming would require enormous resources, the preliminaries are probably still achievable in this century. More complicated is the question of transforming the atmosphere into one that could support human life – this could take centuries, perhaps even millennia. A terraformed Mars could be habitable by early next century if humans living there were prepared to wear breathing apparatus.

▲ Imagined stage-by-stage terraforming of Mars, which may make it possible to inhabit the planet by early next century.

## ⟩ TECH SPEC: TERRAFORMING

- Earth and Mars have very different atmospheric makeups (see table below), so the process of terraforming would require converting the Martian atmosphere to something similar to that on Earth.

Atmospheric composition of Earth and Mars

|  | Earth | Mars |
| --- | --- | --- |
| Nitrogen | 78.1 per cent | 2.7 per cent |
| Oxygen | 20.9 per cent | 0.2 per cent |
| Argon | 0.9 per cent | 1.6 per cent |
| Carbon dioxide and other gases | 0.1 per cent | 95.5 per cent |

- First, the temperature and atmospheric pressure of Mars would need to be increased. This could be triggered in a variety of ways:

  - Releasing greenhouse gases into the atmosphere would heat the surface of the planet by trapping heat.

  - Mirrors orbiting the planet would warm the surface and release $CO_2$, a greenhouse gas.

  - Ammonia-laden asteroids redirected to crash into the planet would release heat and raise the surface temperature.

- The increased temperature would cause the vast quantities of ice on Mars to melt, providing vital water.

- The melting ice ($H_2O$) would also release oxygen ($O_2$) into the atmosphere.

- Oxygen ($O_2$) molecules would absorb ultraviolet radiation in the atmosphere and break into single O atoms, which would then join with other $O_2$ molecules to create $O_3$, ozone. This would help to shield the planet against lethal ultraviolet radiation.

- When a reasonably stable, pressurised and protective atmosphere had been created, microbes and plant life that are sustainable in carbon dioxide environments would be introduced to break down oxygen-containing compounds and release the oxygen into the atmosphere.

- Finally, once the Martian atmosphere had been converted into a breathable state, humans could move in.

# MAGLEV TRAINS ⋰

*Today, if you want to travel from one end of a large country to the other, or get to the other side of the world, your best option is the aeroplane. All this could be about to change: one day in the not-too-distant future we could be travelling at supersonic speeds between major cities on levitating trains, or cruising between continents at hypersonic speeds through vacuum-filled tunnels.*

## ⋰ SCIENTIFIC HISTORY

⋰ As early as 1910, American engineering student Robert Goddard designed a detailed prototype of a 'maglev' (magnetic levitation) train, and also proposed sending the trains through a vacuum-filled tunnel, where these 'vacutrains' would be able to travel even faster due to the lack of air resistance. His designs were only found after his death in 1945. His planned train would have travelled from Boston to New York in 12 minutes, averaging 1,609 kilometres per hour (1,000 miles per hour). However, it wasn't until 1969 that the first patent for a maglev train was issued, and 2002 that the first commercial high-

> **1910_**
>
> Goddard conceives maglev and vacutrains

◀ A Transrapid maglev train car – this company runs the current Shanghai intracity line.

## ⋰ SIGHTINGS IN SCI-FI

- Faster trains were always a given but perhaps because they weren't as fantastic as the jetpack or flying car they weren't given their due until the 1970s, when Larry Niven wrote in *A World Out of Time* that the gravity-assisted train was the fastest intercontinental ground travel possible, reaching speeds past 804 kilometres per hour (500 miles per hour ).

- Movies with futuristic subway scenes include the eerily life-like subway of *The Matrix* (1999), the Spielberg subway of the near-future in *Minority Report* (2002) and the derelict underground system in 2006's *V for Vendetta*.
- Trains involving vacuum tunnels appeared in the German film *Der Tunnel* (1933), remade as the British film *Transatlantic Tunnel* (1935).

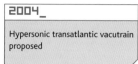

**2004_**

Hypersonic transatlantic vacutrain proposed

**2002_**

First high-speed maglev train, in Shanghai, China

**1984_**

First low-speed maglev train, in Birmingham, UK

**1969_**

First patent for a maglev train issued

◀ A maglev train on display in Munich, Germany.

speed maglev train was introduced as a commuter service in Shanghai, China. There are currently plans to expand the track. Scientists in Japan, Germany and the United States are also expressing interest in the technology: in one scheme, proposed by retired MIT researchers Ernst Frankel and Frank Davidson, a buoyant vacuum tunnel would be anchored across the Atlantic Ocean between North America and Europe, to create a conduit for a hypersonic vacutrain.

## ⠶ REALITY

⠶ Maglev trains are already in use for intracity transit, primarily in Shanghai. The demonstration line in Shanghai transports people 30 kilometres (18.6 miles) to the airport in just 7 minutes 20 seconds, with a top speed of 431 kilometres per hour (268 miles per hour) and an average speed of 254 kilometres per hour (150 miles per hour). Maglev systems are also in development for intercity travel in Germany, the UK and the United States, and similar projects have been proposed between London and Glasgow, Berlin and Hamburg, and several US cities, including Baltimore and Washington, DC. Meanwhile, Japanese-developed maglevs can reach speeds fast enough to travel from Paris to Rome in just 2 hours. Vacutrains – even faster maglev trains that travel through vacuum-filled tunnels – are prohibitively expensive, with estimates of up to US$50 million per mile of tunnel.

However, besides the cost and issues of construction and maintenance, serious safety concerns are holding back this new transit development. Public confidence in maglev trains was rocked when, in 2006, 23 people were killed and 10 injured when a hi-tech driverless magnetic levitation train crashed into a maintenance wagon on a test run in Germany.

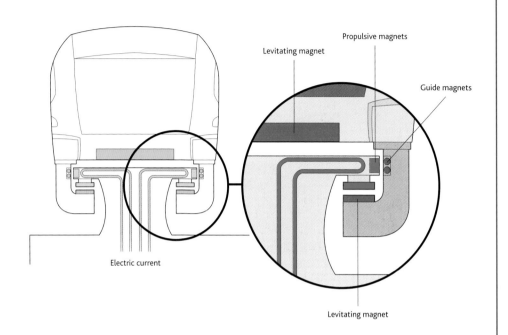

Propulsive magnets

Levitating magnet

Guide magnets

Electric current

Levitating magnet

- A maglev train requires three components to work:
  - A large electric power source.
  - Magnetic coils in the guideway (replacing a track).
  - Large magnets attached to the underside of the train.
- The magnetic coil in the guideway repels the magnets in the underside of the train, causing it to float at up to 10 cm (4 inches) above the guideway.
- The repelling magnetic forces then propel the train forward:
  - The electrical current in the guideway coils alternates, changing the polarity of the coils.
  - This causes the magnetic field in front of the train to pull it forward.

- The magnetic field behind the train adds to the forward thrust.
- Maglev technology is capable of producing speeds of 482–676 kilometres per hour (300–420 miles per hour). As the trains ride on a magnetic field, without any contact with a track, there is no friction with the ground. This means that the trains can move passengers between major centres at the same speed as commuter flights: a trip from Chicago to New York on a maglev train, for example, would take under two hours and use much less fuel than a plane.

# TIME TRAVEL

*Crash your car on the way to work? Don't worry, hop in a time machine, travel back to before the accident and take the subway instead. Want to see how your great grandchild turned out? Pop into the future for his graduation. Be anywhere at any time, past or present, simply by dialling the time and place.*

## ⁘ SCIENTIFIC HISTORY

Einstein's 1915 General Theory of Relativity is the basis for much scientific theory on time travel. Among other things, it suggests that time slows down for objects moving at high speeds, effectively allowing one-way travel to the future at relativistic speeds.

Einstein's theory of relativity also suggests that space and time get pulled out of shape near an accelerated or rotating object. In the 1920s and 1930s several scientists suggested that an infinitely long, dense cylinder spinning at a speed close to the speed of light could be used to warp space-time. Flying a spaceship in a corkscrew around the cylinder, for example, might theoretically allow time

> **1915_**
>
> Albert Einstein's General Theory of Relativity

## ⁘ SIGHTINGS IN SCI-FI

- Time travel made its debut in the public consciousness with H G Wells' novel, *The Time Machine*, in 1895. Since then it has become a popular plot device, used to set a character in a different era, and to explore that character's interaction with the people and technology of that time – a new take on the age-old 'fish out of water' story.

- In blockbuster films such as the *Back to the Future* and *Terminator* trilogies, the heroes go back in time to change the present/future. *Twelve Monkeys* showed a character played by Bruce Willis going back in time to stop someone trying to destroy the world's population with a devastating bioweapon.

travel. In the 1940s Einstein's friend Kurt Gödel theorised that massive objects themselves could cause closed timelike loops, bringing two points in time closer together.

## > REALITY

> In 1975, Einstein's theory of time-dilation was tested by American physicist Carrol Alley. She synchronised two atomic clocks and put one on an aeroplane. Back on the ground, she compared the two. The jet-board clock was microseconds behind the control, suggesting time had slowed fractionally with the speed of the plane. Gödel's ideas were revisited by astrophysicist Richard Gott in 1991. He concluded that closed timelike curves were theoretically possible, and could in the future be used as the basis for travel to the past.

Back on Earth, Ronald Mallet at the University of Connecticut theorised in 2001 that the gravitational field produced by a laser beam could be manipulated to allow time travel. Physicists have long suggested that wormholes might allow instant travel across time as well as space (see pages 36-37). However, physicist Stephen Hawking believes the laws of physics 'conspire to prevent time travel, on a macroscopic scale', and the scientific evidence to refute this has yet to be discovered.

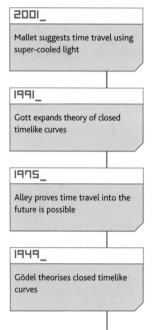

**2001_**
Mallet suggests time travel using super-cooled light

**1991_**
Gott expands theory of closed timelike curves

**1975_**
Alley proves time travel into the future is possible

**1949_**
Gödel theorises closed timelike curves

## > TECH SPEC: TIME TRAVEL THEORY

The University of Connecticut's theoretical physicist Ronald Mallet's work on time travel is based on Einstein's General Theory of Relativity, which states that both matter and energy can create a gravitational field. Therefore, the energy in a light beam can produce a gravitational field, which can be used to warp space-time as follows:

- High-powered lasers are bounced around a rectangle, redirecting the beam of light at each corner until it loops around on itself.

- A second laser is beamed back against the loop and the light is cooled to slow it down using a bath of super-frigid atoms called a Bose–Einstein condensate.

- The intensity of the light is then increased so that space and time swap roles: inside the circulating light beam, time runs round and round, while what to an outsider looks like time becomes like an ordinary dimension of space.

- Scaled to a device used by humans, a time traveller would walk into the swirl of light and therefore back in time. This person, seemingly walking in the right direction, could actually be walking backwards in time as measured outside the circle. So, after walking for a while, you could leave the circle and meet yourself before you entered it.

# WORMHOLES

*Long-haul transoceanic flights to see the Statue of Liberty, or far longer transgalactic trips to see the Plough, could be cut short by opening up a wormhole in space-time and squirting through, cutting travel time from many hours to mere moments or several millennia to months, depending on the distance to your destination.*

## SCIENTIFIC HISTORY

Theoretical physicists have been suggesting the existence of shortcuts for travel through time and space since 1935, when Albert Einstein and his longtime collaborator, Nathan Rosen, published a paper suggesting the existence of mathematical constructs called 'bridges'. The name 'wormhole' was coined in the late 1950s by physicist John Archibald Wheeler, a pioneer in the search for quantum gravity. Wheeler theorised that wormholes would seal themselves off before anything or anyone could get through them. The debate continues to this day, throwing up many questions that science is still unable to answer: How do you find or create a wormhole? How do you keep it open? What would happen if you went through one?

## SIGHTINGS IN SCI-FI

- Wormholes were hypothesised and used by Ellie Arroway to get to the centre of the galaxy in Carl Sagan's novel *Contact* (1985), and have since then become one of the most popular routes of transport and travel in science fiction.

- They have appeared in television series such as *Stargate SG1* and *Stargate Atlantis*, *Star Trek: Deep Space Nine* and *Star Trek: Voyager*.

- Some *Doctor Who* fans have suggested that the Doctor's Tardis travels through a wormhole but the Time Lord has stayed quiet on the subject.

◄ Wormholes in *Star Trek* are used for instant trans-galactic travel.

## ⸭ REALITY

⸭ Wormholes are mathematically possible but beyond the research of our current technology. The most promising is called a Lorentzian wormhole, which opens a portal from any point in the universe to any other point.

If they exist in nature, wormholes are extremely small: based on Einstein's theories, they are $10^{25}$ times smaller than an atom. Once we've found a wormhole, we'll have to work out how to expand it enough for us to travel through.

## ⸭ TECH SPEC: WORMHOLES

- A wormhole is space-time warped in the opposite direction to its natural curvature. At quantum distances (where atoms are planet-size), space-time becomes foamy (turbulent and violently changeable). The bubbles in that foam are probably wormholes.

- To make a wormhole useful, you would have to stretch one of these bubbles massively open so you could crawl into it. However, once inside a wormhole your mass would add positive energy to it, causing it to slam shut. So, to make a wormhole traversable, you would need something to hold it open.

- The solution is something called ghost radiation (sometimes called exotic matter), which is a theoretical negative energy field. This exotic matter could compensate for the positive energy of the mass of the traveller, holding open the wormhole's throat long enough to pop through. The problem is that negative energy is very elusive. A physical force called the Casimir effect – the attractive force between two surfaces in a vacuum – exhibits some qualities suggestive of exotic matter but has been detected only in tiny quantities in the laboratory.

- Even if you could find a way to pour exotic matter into a wormhole to hold it open, you'd need lots of it – the equivalent amount of energy created if you converted the mass of Jupiter (or the mass of 318 Earths).

# COMPUTERS, CYBORGS AND ROBOTS ⁙

Don't panic. The sci-fi nightmare of machines gaining free will and rising up against their masters is unlikely to come true – you might as well worry about a zombie apocalypse. And yet, despite the improbability of a robot rebellion, fears of angry AIs hunting us down tickle the imagination. Science fiction often paints a less-than-rosy picture when computers are involved, whether it's a cyberpunk future where technology robs us of our decency, or a Jetsonian future where robots consent to work for us but mock us at every available opportunity. Perhaps we want to believe in the Terminator or the Matrix out of misplaced masochism: 'human guilt' for our unchecked dominion over machines.

Still, beneath this pessimism lingers a realisation of how dramatically computers have changed our lives for the better over the past few decades, and with that realisation, a longing – or an expectation – for more. Where's all that leisure time we were promised? Shouldn't our factory-ordered butlers and maids have come in by now? As it turns out, help is on the way. We're on the fast track to capitalising on many exciting advances in the fields of computing and robotics, from electronic assistants to save us time, to virtual realities where we can spend the time we've saved.

◀ Darth Vader is one of cinema's iconic cyborg villains.

# ARTIFICIAL INTELLIGENCE ⋖

*In our increasingly virtual world, where business and relationships can easily be conducted with no human contact, the next logical step is artificial intelligence: intelligent behaviour, learning and adaptation in machines. Computer-generated personalities could be assigned to any kind of machine, so you could have a conversation with any computer just as you would a human, or perhaps get revenge on your boss by reprogramming his car with his mother-in-law's personality.*

## ⋗ SCIENTIFIC HISTORY

⋗ Alan Turing opened the debate about the possibility of artificial intelligence in his 1936 paper 'On computable numbers'. Since then, researchers have developed several intelligent programs that can successfully interact with humans and perform tasks autonomously. These have taken several forms, from programs designed to play games such as chess; programs called chatbots, with which a human can have a 'live' typed conversation; and vehicles that can steer and navigate for themselves.

1936_

Alan Turing publishes 'On computable numbers'

The 1980s saw the emergence of 'neural networks', made up of interconnected processors that not only process information but adapt and learn from the patterns they find. The system Cyc uses common sense drawn from millions of simple rules and assertions added to its database by humans to make decisions. Further development into AI has created autonomous systems that can fly aircraft and even spacecraft.

In order to boost research into AI, in 2004 the Defense Advanced Research Projects Agency (DARPA), the central research organisation of the US Department of Defense, introduced an annual prize

◀ Max Headroom, of the eponymous late 1980s TV series featuring an AI newscaster.

competition for driverless cars. Entrants in the first DARPA Grand Challenge engineered intelligent autonomous vehicles that navigated a course in the Mojave Desert. Although none of the vehicles finished the 229-kilometre (142-mile) route that year, by 2005 five vehicles made their way to the finish line with no human input during the journey.

## SIGHTINGS IN SCI-FI

- In the 1960s, the *Star Trek* computer was given a human voice and an absolutely logical personality, something the malfunctioning and murderous HAL 9000 made up for in Arthur C Clarke's 1968 novel *2001: A Space Odyssey*.

- In the 1980s, Max Headroom appeared in the eponymous television series: a wise-cracking AI who could move through computers and televisions at will.

- Also that decade, the talking car KITT (standing for Knight Industries Two Thousand) was David Hasselhoff's electronic sidekick in the TV series *Knight Rider*.

- Perhaps the most famous computer-generated personality of recent years is the sinister Agent Smith in the *Matrix* movies of 1999–2003.

▲ The Stanford Racing Team's robot car, 'Stanley,' won the 2005 DARPA Grand Challenge by completing a 229-km (132-mile) off-road desert course in the fastest time, less than 7 hours.

## 1980s_

Neural networks emerge

## 1997_

Deep Blue beats world chess champion Garry Kasparov

## 1999_

NASA hands over control of *Deep Space 1* to an AI system

## 2001_

OpenCyc is made available on the Internet

## › REALITY

› AI systems are already in use today, mainly in the fields of banking, finance and information technology (IT). Banks use AI systems to invest in stocks and manage properties, businesses use the technology to organise schedules and staff, and credit card companies use AI to sniff out fraud. 'Chatbots' are common on the Internet, although if you spend any time with them you'll end up frustrated as they respond in gibberish to any but the simplest of questions. However, basic AI is used every day by Internet search engines like Ask.com, which can make sense of typed questions and respond with reasonably useful answers.

Alan Turing set the standard by which AI is judged in 1950, when he conceived the Turing Test – a truly intelligent machine must be able to hold a conversation with a person, without that person being aware that he/she is talking to a computer. Technology still has a long way to go before human intelligence is indistinguishable from artificial intelligence but in 2006, AI visionary Ray Kurzweil – who has successfully predicted many AI developments of recent years – predicted that a computer will pass the Turing Test by 2029.

## 2001_

Unmanned *Global Hawk* flies from California to Australia

## 2007_

The DARPA Challenge moves to a realistic urban context

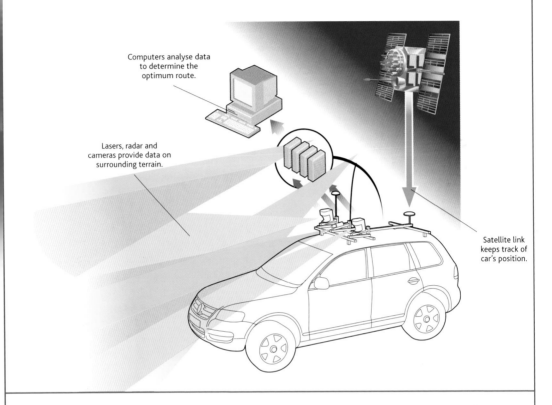

Computers analyse data
to determine the
optimum route.

Lasers, radar and
cameras provide data on
surrounding terrain.

Satellite link
keeps track of
car's position.

The winning vehicle in the 2005 DARPA challenge was an AI–powered Volkswagen Touareg, modified by the Stanford Racing Team (SRT) at Stanford University. SRT called their vehicle 'Stanley' and assert that its success came largely from well-engineered AI software that runs on 7 Pentium M computers:

- Two Global Positioning System (GPS) antennae, an inertial measurement system and wheel speed measurements generate positioning data for the car.

- Five laser range finders, radar and a camera system allow Stanley to 'see' obstacles.

- The AI software maps the terrain around the car to determine if it is in one of three states: drivable, not drivable or unknown.

All of these data inputs are analysed by different programs running on the synchronised computers. A key element of the software is a Kalman filter, a program which brings raw data together, analyses it and predicts how it will change in the future. In Stanley's software, the filter uses the data gathered from the car's sensors and computers to judge what state the vehicle is in and to make predictions as to how that state will change in the future. The software then plans a path and commands the car to follow that path, with adjustments being made as and when new data comes in.

# ROBOT PETS ⋱

*If you love animals but hate litter boxes or are allergic to fur, an artificial pet might be what you're looking for. There's no need to worry about getting home on time to feed it or arranging for someone to look after it while you're on holiday – simply turn it off whenever it's inconvenient!*

## ⋮ SCIENTIFIC HISTORY

The first robotic pet appeared in 1738, when French engineer Jacques de Vaucanson designed a mechanical duck with 400 moving parts that could eat, flap its wings and excrete. The first commercial success in this area came a couple of centuries later, in 1997, with the invention of the Tamagotchi. Owners had to keep their portable, on-screen pets happy by feeding them, playing with them, and cleaning them, all by pressing a series of buttons. In terms of robot pets, Tiger Electronics' Furby has probably been the most successful. The soft toy has expressive motorised eyes and a limited vocabulary that improves over time.

## ⋮ SIGHTINGS IN SCI-FI

- The 1970s saw the first robot pet when K-9, a robot dog and every Time Lord's best friend, appeared on the original *Doctor Who* television series.

- In the 1980s, *C.O.P.S.* featured a robot police dog, Blitz, as part of a K-9000 robot dog unit.

- In *Blade Runner* (1982), we meet 'Animoids,' genetically engineered replicas of extinct species kept as pets or beasts of burden.

- And, as so often happens, everything old becomes new again: in the 2002 film *Jimmy Neutron: Boy Genius*, Jimmy has a best friend and companion in Goddard, his robotic dog.

▲ Sony's AIBO 110 (right) and 210 (left), released in 1999 and 2000 respectively.

## ⸭ REALITY

⸭ The robotic pets and companions available today tend to be toys rather than replacements for their biological equivalents. Sony's robo-dog AIBO is perhaps the best-known robotic companion, released in various models from 1999.

Mitsubishi has also developed a US$1 million robotic replica of the extinct coelacanth, a fish species that died out millions of years ago. It has been suggested that realistic models of extinct animals could be used in exhibits in museums and aquariums. Research like this suggests robotic fish for a home fishtank – as seen in the TV series *Red Dwarf* – could be available soon.

## ⸭ TECH SPEC: PLEO

California-based robotics company Ugobe released a robot pet dinosaur in late 2006. The genius of Pleo, which resembles a one-week-old baby dinosaur from the Late Jurassic period, lies in its apparently spontaneous responses and fluid movements. These are achieved thanks to 38 sensors that detect light, motion, touch and sound.

- The robot's operating system uses eight processors that can handle up to 60 million calculations per second. This allows the robot to respond to and interact with people and the surrounding environment.

- Fourteen servo joints in Pleo's head, neck, legs, torso and tail can sense if the robot is being restrained: as a result, Pleo can walk, back up, detect edges and avoid obstacles.

- A light sensor allows it to differentiate night from day.

# HUMANOIDS AND ARTIFICIAL PEOPLE ⋮

*Robots that can move like humans have hundreds of possible uses but the thought of artificial people that are indistinguishable from humans walking among us is slightly scary. Given the rate at which technology advances, and given current developments in artificial intelligence, some are concerned that these artifical people could eventually become superior to human beings.*

## ⋮ SCIENTIFIC HISTORY

⋮ The history of humanoid robots has been dominated by Japan. Human-like robots that can walk, see and speak have been around for decades – starting with the first bipedal humanoid robot, WABOT, which was developed at Waseda University in Tokyo. These robots have assumed ever more human properties since then. In 2000, Honda revealed ASIMO, a humanoid robot that walks on two legs with a surprisingly human gait. More recently, Repliee Q1,

## ⋮ SIGHTINGS IN SCI-FI

- Isaac Asimov pioneered the idea of robots gaining intelligence and rebelling against being mere workers in his series of robot stories and novels of the 1940s and 50s, on which the movies *Bicentennial Man* (1999) and *I, Robot* (2004) are based. According to the Oxford English Dictionary, Asimov even coined the term 'robotics' in 1942.

- Philip K Dick changed our perception of how 'human' an android is in his 1968 novel *Do Androids Dream of Electric Sheep?*

- In *Blade Runner*, the groundbreaking 1982 film, Rick Deckard (played by Harrison Ford) tracks and destroys androids, before being forced to confront their – and his own – humanity.

unveiled in 2005 at Osaka University in Japan, has lifelike silicone skin and can mimic gestures such as eye blinks, speaking and breathing. The robot – known as an Actroid – can understand 400 words, while tiny motors in its silicone face give the robot the ability to express joy, anger and sorrow.

## REALITY

Although the androids and gynoids (female androids) developed so far may look like, and sometimes express themselves like, humans, they currently have very limited speech and motion abilities. While both Repliee and the Korean Institute of Industrial Technology's EveR-1 (released in 2006) demonstrate huge steps forward in the development of artificial humans, their vocabularies are limited and both are fixed in a sitting position. However, advances in robot mobility in Japan, especially the work done by Honda on ASIMO, could be added to create walking Actroids, while developments in artificial intelligence (see pages 40–43) could allow them to become autonomous (most experimental walking robots are currently controlled via wireless commands).

Research carried out in 2006 suggests that autonomous humanoid robots, designed for public use, are a decade away; but humanoid robots that are completely indistinguishable from humans are not likely to be available soon. Artificial humans may be a reality later this century but remain science fiction for now.

▲ The humanoid robot Actroid Repliee on display at the 2005 World Exposition in Japan.

## TECH SPEC: ASIMO

Perhaps the most advanced humanoid robot is Honda's ASIMO, a 1.2-metre (4-foot) tall machine with a spookily human gait. Honda robot scientists developed this remarkable mobility by studying human movements. ASIMO can copy these movements using a speed sensor and a gyroscope, and can use all of its onboard technology to run at 3 kmh (1.8 mph), walk up and down stairs, and perform smooth walking turns by shifting its centre of gravity.

- The gyroscope measures body position and orientation.

- The speed sensor measures how fast ASIMO is moving.

- This information is sent to ASIMO's onboard computer, allowing it to make adjustments to the robot's joints on the fly.

- The robot's feet, which have toe-like shock absorbers, assist with balance and compensate for any uneven ground.

- The information from the gyroscope allows ASIMO to adjust its torso in the opposite direction to the start of a fall to compensate for imbalance.

# ENTERTAINMENT
# SYSTEMS ∴

*Simulated entertainment systems open a whole new world of possibility. Imagine being able to generate any scenario you want, in a form that is indistinguishable from reality: you could fight outlaws in the Wild West, play baseball with Babe Ruth, or just enjoy all the unhealthy food you can eat without experiencing any of the side effects.*

## ⸬ SCIENTIFIC HISTORY

⸬ The vast majority of research and development in virtual entertainment has focused on computer and video games, from a computer version of Tic Tac Toe to the opening of HoloDek, a state-of-the-art gaming facility including lifesized monitors with surround-sound audio systems. The technology behind the prototype virtual reality environment *Virtusphere*, unveiled in 1997, has even been considered for military training.

## ⸬ SIGHTINGS IN SCI-FI

• William Gibson introduced the world to cyberspace and virtual reality in stories and novels such as *Neuromancer* (1984).

• Neal Stephenson coined the term 'avatar' in the 1992 novel *Snow Crash* to describe one's identity in the virtual world.

• *Star Trek: The Next Generation* (1987–1994) popularised the holodeck, a virtual reality facility that allowed users to re-create and experience anything they wanted. The series also suggested ways the technology might backfire – for example, Professor Moriarty coming to life from a virtual Sherlock Holmes adventure.

• In the *X-Men* comics, the heroes trained in the Danger Room, which started out as a collection of real weapons but evolved into something more like the holodeck in the 2006 movie *X-Men III: The Last Stand*.

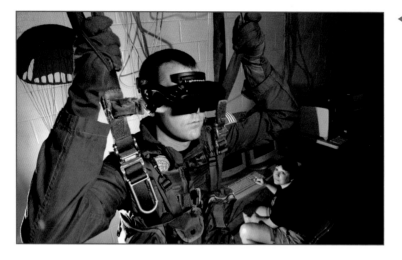

## > REALITY

> While elements of the holodeck are possible today, others still have a long way to go. While 2D holograms exist, for example, 3D holograms don't, and the force fields required to make a hologram *feel* real are still science-fiction. Nevertheless, surround-sound and photo-realistic graphics are increasingly common in cinema and video games and the technology is improving all the time.

## > TECH SPEC: HOLODECKS

Holodecks would work in the following way:

- In the distance you see a large chocolate cake on a picnic table (projected video image on a wall).
- You walk towards it (on a force field treadmill) and walk around it (3D hologram).
- Then you sit down at the table (3D holograms combined with force beams to make a solid object).
- Finally, you take a piece of cake (replicated) and eat it.

Scientists are still some way from achieving all of the above. Perhaps the closest thing to a holodeck today is immersive game technology developed at the Helsinki University of Technology in Finland, and commercialised by Finland-based Animaatiokone Industries. The researchers developed a game called

*Kick Ass Kung Fu* that lets players fight onscreen enemies using real kicks, punches or acrobatic fighting moves. Players can also use real props such as axes or swords to fight the video opponents.

- The game is played on a 5-metre (15-foot) cushioned play space in front of one or more large video screens.
- A video camera captures the players' movements.
- The camera then superimposes the players' movements onto an onscreen silhouette.
- The game computer then adapts the captured moves to one of a catalogue of onscreen moves, which is then displayed by a player's character in the game in real time.

# AI MARKETING ⠶

*Our environment already seems saturated with advertisements clamouring for our attention, so a world where ads can target their message specifically to you may not be a future you want to envision. Identifying you by a chip you carry in your wallet, advertising billboards will be able to address you in person, after assessing how likely it is that you'll be interested in their product.*

## ⠶ SCIENTIFIC HISTORY

⠶ The technology that would allow advertising billboards to identify a person has been around since 1973, when scientists at Los Alamos Scientific Laboratory unveiled Radio Frequency Identification (RFID) tags – tiny chips that can be scanned using radio waves to identify the person or product that carries them. However, the problem has been persuading consumers to carry the chips so that they can be identified. Perhaps the closest real-world equivalent is Amazon.com's A9 search engine, released in 2004, which records customers' searches and purchases and connects them with other searches in their accounts to make recommendations of other similar products that might interest them.

1973_

RFID tags demonstrated at Los Alamos laboratory

## ⠶ SIGHTINGS IN SCI-FI

• A common theme in sci-fi is that everything around us will get smarter thanks to artificial intelligence, so that brands will be able to target you specifically through their marketing, advertising and point-of-purchase campaigns.

• This is brilliantly illustrated in the 2002 movie *Minority Report*, when John Anderton (played by Tom Cruise) is trying to walk through a mall anonymously, only to be constantly identified and called out to by computerised advertising wall mounts.

## ⸬ REALITY

⸬ The technology exists today to make smart billboards happen. A company called Thinking Pictures is in the business of interactive displays, with networked plasma screens fitted with stereo speakers and a series of sensors that can detect people nearby. When the screen senses someone in its proximity, the display runs an animation or audio message. Some boards are equipped with a touch screen so potential consumers can interact with the ad. Other technologies can be used to interact further with a potential customer: screens can be equipped with Bluetooth, a short-range wireless technology available in many mobile phones, to identify a passing phone and send advertising data to it by text message. Barcode or magnetic card readers, or RFID sensors can also be used to identify passersby, if they can be persuaded to stop and let the machine identify them.

The biggest roadblock to having a personalised experience with smart ads is the issue of privacy: marketers cannot be sure that consumers are going to want to have their name appear on a public ad as they come near it. However, loyalty cards combined with incentives might be used to entice a user to interact with an ad.

Meanwhile, Google's CEO, Eric Schmidt, has said that one day soon customised radio ads that work with in-car GPS will alert you to deals and buying opportunities based on your car's location, broadcast through the car radio.

**2005_**
Bell and Pizza send promotions by text message

**2004_**
Amazon.com releases A9 search engine

**1998_**
Nightclubs in the US use RFID to identify VIP clients

**1994_**
First Internet banner advert

## ⸬ TECH SPEC: AI ADVERTISING

For AI advertising to work, the advertising display device needs to recognise you. This identification process can be achieved using an RFID (Radio Frequency Identification) tag, a tiny low-cost chip with an antenna that you can either wear or keep in your wallet. There are two types of RFID tags: active tags have their own battery, which allows them to be identified even at a distance from the RFID reader, while passive tags are unpowered, and have a range of less than 2.5 centimetres (an inch).

- The ad display sends out radio waves that are recognised by the tag.

- The tag responds with its own radio signal, conveying information to a reader in the advertising display. This data exchange occurs in less than a tenth of a second.

- The data reflected to the reader is usually a numeric address that can be cross-referenced in a database to retrieve information about the carrier of the RFID tag and adjust the message accordingly.

If RFID tags were adapted for use in everyday life, interactive ads, with your permission, could give you a customised advertising experience as you came into contact with them.

# POCKET COMPUTERS ⠿

*Early computers took up entire rooms, so the pioneers of IT would never have believed that all of that processing technology and more could be compressed into a handheld device – much less one on which you could jot notes as if on a pad of paper or one you could command by voice.*

## ⠿ SCIENTIFIC HISTORY

⠿ Pocket-sized 'computers' first came onto the market in the 1970s but they should have more accurately been called calculators due to their limited functions. The technology required to run a computer has become increasingly minute, however, since Timex Seiko's tiny Timex Sinclair 1000, launched in 1982 and USRobotics' PalmPilot, introduced in 1996.

With the advent of the Internet, mobile phones and wireless technology, the potential uses for pocket computers have sky-rocketed. The idea that you could not only make phone calls but send e-mails, review documents, and browse the Internet all from a terminal small enough to fit in your pocket has obvious appeal to

## ⠿ SIGHTINGS IN SCI-FI

- Bigger was better for early computers in sci-fi and popular culture, and they originally appeared as rooms full of flickering lights.

- The pocket computer was pioneered in *Star Trek* (1966) in the form of a tricorder, a handheld computer that could perform scientific and medical scanning, and data analysis.

- The first reference to a pocket computer with a stylus was in the novel *The Mote in God's Eye*, by Larry Niven and Jerry Pournelle (1974).

the globe-trotting modern businessman or woman. Today, computing and telecommunications technology are combined in the same device, allowing users to carry everything they need for work and personal life in their pocket.

There is a downside to these developments: by the early 2000s, many people had become so addicted to their BlackBerrys that they became known as 'crackberries'.

## ⸬ REALITY

⸬ If there was ever a science fiction idea that has been realised, it's the pocket computer. Today, for less than £500, you can buy a device that fulfils most of sci-fi's dreams. Pocket computers, or PDAs (personal digital assistants), have processing power that is thousands of times faster than their room-sized ancestors. Handheld devices from Palm Inc, Hewlett Packard and Nokia, to name a few, run software, play back audio and video and recognise handwriting, while higher-end versions (also referred to as smartphones) also wirelessly connect to the Internet and can even record and play video. Some pocket computers can understand simple spoken commands and as the speed of mobile microprocessors increases, so does the complexity of the commands they can understand.

As the technology required to store and process data becomes increasingly miniaturised, there seems to be no limit to what can be accomplished using a remarkably tiny piece of electronics. Future versions could be combined with retinal projectors (see pages 74–77), video-phones (see pages 72–73) and instant connection to data storage across the globe, to create a pocket-sized office that operates anywhere in the world.

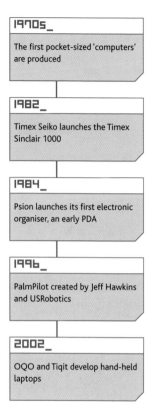

**1970s_**

The first pocket-sized 'computers' are produced

**1982_**

Timex Seiko launches the Timex Sinclair 1000

**1984_**

Psion launches its first electronic organiser, an early PDA

**1996_**

PalmPilot created by Jeff Hawkins and USRobotics

**2002_**

OQO and Tiqit develop hand-held laptops

## ⸬ TECH SPEC: PDAs

Pocket computers consist of four key elements:

- A mobile microprocessor paired with memory chips provides the device's processing capabilities. PDA processors run at around half a gigahertz; San Francisco-based OQO offers a palm-sized computer, the 001+, which runs at 1 GHz.

- Data is displayed on a small high-resolution colour LCD screen.

- The devices are powered by a lithium ion battery that works for days on standby or for several hours while in continuous use.

- Wireless components connect the device to the Internet over a short-range Wi-Fi network. These Wi-Fi hotspots are available in airports and coffee bars, at home or on business premises. Some devices also access the Internet over high-speed cellular data networks.

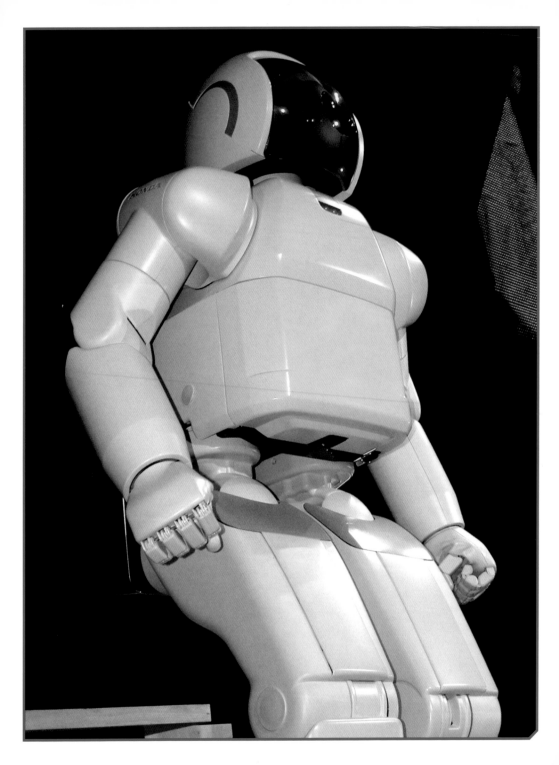

# ROBOT HELPER ⋖

*Cleaning, looking after the kids, walking the dog – it's all such a chore. Think about all the spare time you'd have if you had a robot maid to run your home, keep it clean, babysit the children and perhaps even walk the pets.*

## ⋗ SCIENTIFIC HISTORY

⋗ Leonardo da Vinci displayed his uncanny knack for predicting future inventions in 1495, when he came up with a design for a mechanical knight. But over the centuries, the kind of help we look for from a robot has changed somewhat. Machines that can mow the lawn and vacuum the carpet for you are already on the market, while products in development include companion and helper robots for the elderly, and robots that can guard your home. Surely robots to walk your robot pets can't be far behind!

> **1495_**
>
> Leonardo da Vinci designs a mechanical knight

◀ Honda's ASIMO humanoid robot might one day do your housework for you.

## ⋗ SIGHTINGS IN SCI-FI

- Although a nanny robot was introduced by science-fiction writer Philip K Dick in a story from the 1950s, it wasn't until Rosie the Robot appeared on *The Jetsons* that the idea of a robot housekeeper caught on in popular culture.

- In the original *Star Trek* TV series of the 1960s, the robot M4 was designed and constructed to serve as a personal housekeeper, sentry and handyman.

- More recently, the films *Bicentennial Man* and *I, Robot* – both based on stories by Isaac Asimov – have warned of the possible rebellion of robot help. In *Bicentennial Man* a robot starts to display signs of intelligence and creativity, while *I, Robot* tells the story of a robot who evolves to sentience and leads other robots against servitude.

◀ Computer rendering of a robot vacuuming – could this be in our near future?

## ▷ REALITY

▷ Of all the single-task house-cleaning robots on the market today, the most widely available model is a vacuum cleaner. These (usually) pie-shaped devices, priced anywhere from a few hundred pounds to £1,000, autonomously trundle around the home vacuuming up dirt and are designed to augment a cleaning routine, not replace it.

An equally ingenious, though possibly more annoying, invention is Clocky, an alarm clock that sounds the wake-up alarm and then rolls away so you have to get out of your bed to turn it off. The device finds new places to hide each time.

Given the popularity of single-task home robots, it's likely that multi-tasking home robots will be developed in the next few years. Already, Mitsubishi Heavy Industries has developed Wakamaru, a 1-metre (3-foot)-tall, 30-kilogram (66-pound) humanoid robot on wheels that can recognise 10 faces and understand 10,000 words. Among other abilities, it can manage your calendar and guard your home, sending an e-mail if it detects motion in the house. Meanwhile, Nursebot, a research project at the University of Pittsburgh and Carnegie Mellon University, aims to develop helper robots for the elderly by operating appliances, monitoring the patient's health and reminding them about personal tasks. Research in Japan suggests that consumer-priced humanoid robo-helpers are likely to be available in the next decade.

**1994_**

Udi Peless develops a lawn-cutting robot

**2001-02_**

iRobot's Roomba and Electrolux's Trilobite on the market

**2005_**

Mitsubishi release Wakamaru, a companion robot

**2006_**

Friendly Robotics introduces Friendly Vac

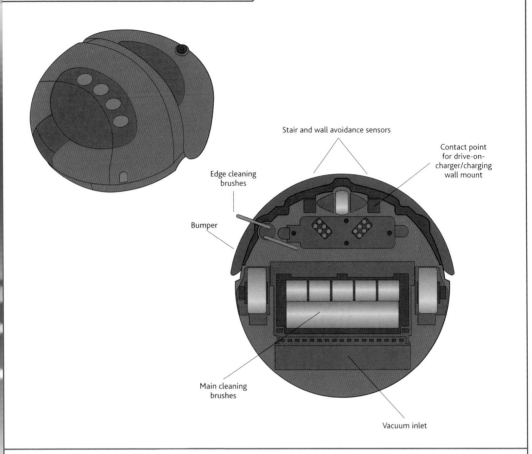

Stair and wall avoidance sensors

Contact point for drive-on-charger/charging wall mount

Edge cleaning brushes

Bumper

Main cleaning brushes

Vacuum inlet

Roomba, iRobot's artificially intelligent vacuuming robot, autonomously navigates through spaces of varying complexity.

- The Roomba has five motors. Two drive its wheels and the remaining three drive the vacuum, a spinning side brush and a rolling agitator.

- It also has a microprocessor brain that calculates an optimal route for cleaning a room. It starts by cleaning in an expanding spiral, but when it hits an obstacle such as furniture it interprets it as the perimeter of a room and begins to clean the outside edges.

- On the underside of the unit, four infrared sensors detect edges, which stop it from falling down stairs. It bounces infrared light continuously at the floor and, if the light doesn't bounce back as expected, it interprets that as a 'cliff' it can fall over and backs off.

- Sensors in the robot's bumpers detect impacts against obstacles. They can also sense the robot's proximity to walls, so it can vacuum close to the skirting board or piece of furniture.

- If it encounters a particularly dirty area of the room, sensors mounted above the brushes turn the device toward the dirt and clean the area more thoroughly.

# WETWARE AND NEUROCHIPS ∵

*Wetware, or software for the brain, could be used to improve your life. Forget about taking the time to learn a foreign language before your holiday. Instead, simply plug a chip into your brain and you'll instantly be able to speak the language of your choice. Say good-bye to last-minute cramming for exams.*

## ∵ SCIENTIFIC HISTORY

∵ The pioneering work of Jose Delgado, who in the 1950s and 1960s successfully treated epilepsy and schizophrenia by implanting electrodes in the brains of animals and humans, paved the way for modern brain implants.

In 1991, scientist Peter Fromherz and his team at the Max Planck Institute for Biochemistry in Germany successfully interfaced leech nerve cells with semiconductor chips; two years later, Fromherz and his colleague Martin Jenkner grew networks of six living snail

## ∵ SIGHTINGS IN SCI-FI

- Wetware devices were first introduced in the novels of William Gibson, where some characters could use a 'cyberdeck' to jack into a brain implant, providing them with sensorial connection to virtual cyberspace.

- More recently, Peter F Hamilton's *Night's Dawn* trilogy featured characters with cybernetic brain implants, which make them super-fast or super-strong or provide an Internet connection through devices in the skin.

- In *Star Trek: Voyager* (1995), the character Seven of Nine had physical and mental enhancements implanted by the Borg, some of which she retained when she joined *Voyager*'s crew.

◀ In the cyber world of the *Matrix*, the hero, played by Keanu Reeves, downloads martial arts skills directly into his brain.

neurons onto silicon chips, demonstrating that cells and chips could communicate. By 2006, Fromherz and his team had developed a neurochip made of silicon and rat tissue. Good news for rats, perhaps, but how about you and your foreign holiday?

## ⊱ REALITY

⊱ Although research is underway to develop neuron–silicon interfaces, the technology required to transfer data in and out of the brain is still a way off. Implants that can replace the functions of a damaged brain are under development: researchers have successfully created an artificial hippocampus – the part of the brain that retains new, long-term memories – for rats. Researcher Ted Berger at the University of Southern California hopes this technology will one day help repair the brains of Alzheimer sufferers or brain-damaged stroke victims.

## ⊱ TECH SPEC: NEUROCHIPS

The most recent scientific development is the creation of a neurochip made out of silicon and rat tissue by researchers at the Max Planck Institute for Biochemistry in Germany, in conjunction with mobile chip maker Infineon.

• They put 16,384 transistors and hundreds of capacitors on a 1mm square chip and then 'glued' rat brain cells to the chip using brain proteins.

• Transistors on the chip could then detect tiny changes in an electric charge when the neurons fired. The electrical charge changes when sodium ions move in and out of the neurons through special cellular openings.

• Meanwhile the capacitors could send impulses back to the neurons. To achieve the communication, the scientists had to genetically enhance the neurons to increase the number of openings.

# CYBERNETICS ⸪

*The development of bionic body parts, prosthetics and artificial organs holds great hope for the future. Traumatic accidents and life-threatening diseases will no longer be a problem – simply pop into the hospital and have a leg, liver or other body part replaced with a mechanical version, then carry on with your life as before.*

## ⸫ SCIENTIFIC HISTORY

⸫ Artificial body parts have been used in medical research since the late 19th century. Amputees in the First World War received the 'Belgian prosthesis', an artificial leg that reproduced the natural look of a leg and was fitted to the residual limb. But it wasn't until 1942 that an artifical mechanism was used to keep an animal alive and not until 1958 that the first mechanical device was implanted into a human body, with the development of cardiac pacemakers to treat heart disease.

Since then, medical science has progressed in leaps and bounds: in 2001, a man who had lost his arms in an accident was provided with bionic arms that he controls using his brain. Transplant techniques have also come a long way since the first successful organ transplant in 1954. The year 1998 saw the first hand transplant and by 2005 scientists were able to offer a partial face transplant – including mouth and nose – to a woman whose face had been ravaged by her dog. But perhaps the most exciting developments are in the worlds of cloning and genetic engineering (see pages 138–141 and 144–147 respectively): between 1999 and 2001, six people were given new bladders that had been grown from their own tissue, thus dramatically reducing the risk that the body would reject the new organs, and in 2006, a rabbit received an artificial penis grown from its own cells.

1885_

First artificial heart-lung used to study blood flow

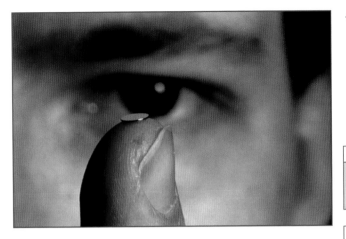

An experimental retinal implant – a semiconductor chip designed to give sight to the blind.

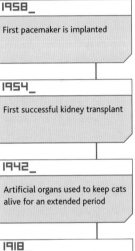

**1958_**

First pacemaker is implanted

**1954_**

First successful kidney transplant

**1942_**

Artificial organs used to keep cats alive for an extended period

**1918_**

The first prosthetic leg, the 'Belgian prosthesis'

## > REALITY

> Transplant science is pretty advanced today, allowing the replacement of many major organs as well as skin, bone and other tissue. The recipient of a partial face transplant in 2005 retained her ability to smoke a cigarette; health concerns aside, the fact that she retained the necessary muscular control was seen as a breakthrough.

Despite widespread transplant successes over the last few decades, some critical problems remain: recipients outnumber donors and recipients' bodies can reject donor organs – the immune system recognises the implanted cells as foreign and attacks them, destroying the new organ. However, new developments in technology allow scientists to grow organs in the lab from the

## > SIGHTINGS IN SCI-FI

- An early reference to artificial organs is the surgically implanted artificial eye in *Galactic Patrol*, written by E E 'Doc' Smith in 1937. However, five years later, Aldous Huxley had already described artificial womb machinery as the source for new citizens in *Brave New World*.

- In 1964, Philip K Dick made reference to artificial metal teeth welded to the bone of the main character in *The Three Stigmata of Palmer Eldritch*. A few years later in *Dune Messiah*, Frank Herbert described the 'insect-like' artificial eyes created by the Tleilaxu.

- *Enterprise* captain Jean-Luc Picard had an artificial heart implanted in the 24th century (in the *Star Trek* universe), and Barry Morse's character in the 1975–1977 British television series *Space: 1999* also had an artificial heart; he wore a watch-like device on his wrist to control it.

▲ The AbioCor is the world's first completely self-contained replacement heart, designed to fully sustain the body's circulatory system.

**1961_**

Three patients regain hearing using cochlear implants

**1982_**

First artificial heart, the 'Jarvik-7', is implanted

**1987_**

First successful whole-lung transplant

**1999–2001_**

Six people receive bladders grown in the lab

**2006_**

A rabbit receives an artificially-grown penis

recipient's own cells, which the patient's immune system recognises as part of the host body and so does not attack.

As for implants and prosthetics, cochlear implants, also known as 'bionic ears', restore hearing in the deaf by wiring a hearing device directly into the auditory nerve, bypassing the ear. Bionic eyes are also being developed: the first experimental eye was implanted in 2000 and clinical trials of a new eye technology, in which a chip implanted in the retina receives images from a video camera mounted on a pair of goggles, are planned in the near future. Artificial hearts also exist, although they are not yet widely used as permanent replacements for biological hearts. The most successful artificial heart is called AbioCor and extends life in recipients by an average of five months, and in one patient as long as 512 days.

As for limbs, scientists are using implants to give amputees the ability to control prosthetic limbs with their minds (see pages 132–134). Meanwhile, researchers funded by the US Department of Veterans' Affairs are working on biohybrid limbs. The idea is to combine man-made components with human tissue to enable prostheses to work like fully functioning human legs and arms.

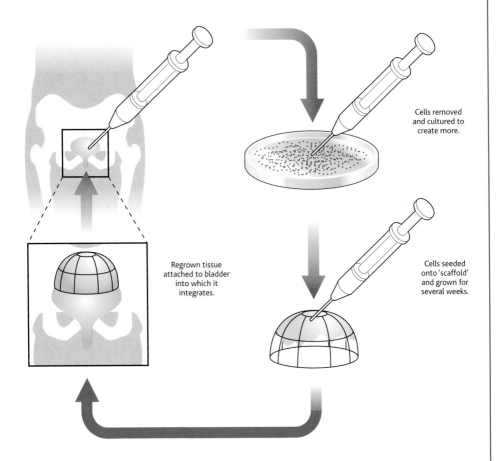

Cells removed and cultured to create more.

Cells seeded onto 'scaffold' and grown for several weeks.

Regrown tissue attached to bladder into which it integrates.

Dr Anthony Atala and his team at the Wake Forest Institute for Regenerative Medicine created and implanted artificial bladders in seven young patients between 1999 and 2001 – the first time tissue engineering had been used to rebuild a complex internal organ in humans.

- To grow a bladder in the lab, scientists first take a sample of the patient's own bladder, including muscle cells and cells from the bladder lining.

- These cells are put on a biodegradable bladder-shaped scaffold made of collagen – a strong tensile protein that makes up 40 per cent of the human body – and left to grow for about two months.

- The bladder is engineered in layers. Cells are laid down and then incubated so they will multiply: one million cells are initially harvested to seed the new bladder and they grow to about 1.5 billion cells in the regenerated organ.

- The resulting organ does not include the top part of the bladder that connects to the kidneys. This is left intact after the old bladder is removed, and used to attach to the new bladder.

# CYBORGS ‹:

*If you're not satisfied with what Mother Nature gave you, use technology to create a superior version of yourself. Part human and part machine, cyborgs – 'cybernetic organisms' – will be able to out-perform regular humans for whichever task they've been designed.*

## › SCIENTIFIC HISTORY

Technologically enhanced humans are not new. You could say that recipients of cochlear implants, first used in 1961, or pacemakers, invented in 1950, are early cyborgs. But arguably, the first cyborgs – integrating machines into their everyday lives – were the women who wore the first wristwatches invented by Patek Phililipe in the late 19th century.

Super-humanism through attached *computer*, rather than mechanical, technology is a relatively recent phenomenon. One of the pioneers is Steve Mann, who in 1981 built a wearable computer, called WearComp, which he has adapted over the years and wears throughout his daily life. The MIT graduate, now a professor at the University of Toronto, is considered the father of wearable computers and is a self-professed cyborg. Kevin Warwick, another experimental cyborg, had a chip implanted in his arm in 1998, which communicated with a central computer system to turn on lights, open doors and control heaters at the University of Reading in England. In 2002, 100 electrodes were implanted into the nerve fibres of his left arm. This array allows him to control an intelligent artificial arm and an electric wheelchair.

More recently, in 2003, Miguel Nicolelis implanted a chip in a monkey's brain that gave it the ability to control a robotic arm.

◄ Artist's impression of cyborg components that could be used to rebuild or enhance a human body.

**1958_**

First pacemaker is implanted

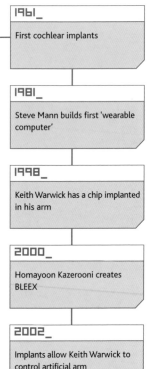

**1961_**
First cochlear implants

**1981_**
Steve Mann builds first 'wearable computer'

**1998_**
Keith Warwick has a chip implanted in his arm

**2000_**
Homayoon Kazerooni creates BLEEX

**2002_**
Implants allow Keith Warwick to control artificial arm

## ⇲ REALITY

⇲ Cyborg science is still relatively new and is unlikely to be available to consumers for another decade or so. However, if you want a hardwired experience sooner then you may want to volunteer to be scientist Miguel Nicolelis's next monkey. By 2009, Dr Nicolelis intends to implant a chip into a human brain that will allow a person to control a robotic arm just by thinking. In time, this research may be the long-awaited key to mechanical augmentation of the human body.

Not quite ready for surgery? Keep an eye on cyborg Steve Mann: the WearComp he wears is always on and gives him a constant connection to computer resources and the Internet. The contraption projects information into his eye, giving him the experience of a world overlaid with computer-enhanced information. He says this layer of information processing could also be used to recognise unwelcome intrusions such as advertising in the real world and blot them out.

Then there's BLEEX (Berkeley Lower Extremities Exoskeleton), a wearable robotic system that allows its wearer to carry up to 90 kilograms (200 pounds) as if it were 4.5 kilograms (10 pounds). BLEEX was invented by Homayoon Kazerooni, director of the Robotics and Human Engineering Laboratory at the University of California, Berkeley, and is funded by the Defense Advanced Research Projects Agency (DARPA), the research arm of the US Department of Defense. It will be used initially for military applications but could also be used by firefighters to protect them from heat and falling debris and help them carry unconscious victims to safety.

## ⇲ SIGHTINGS IN SCI-FI

- Martin Caidin's novel *Cyborg* was a bestseller in 1972; it was later adapted into the television programme *The Six Million Dollar Man*, which spread the idea of 'bionics' – and of overcoming natural limitations with artificial organs.

- In the world of *Star Wars*, Darth Vader is a cyborg. Even Luke Skywalker is arguably a minor cyborg when he gets an artificial hand attached.

- The 1987 movie and the spin-off television series *RoboCop* gave us a policeman whose brain, face and other organic parts were attached to a life-support system inside a human-shaped titanium body: essentially, a machine with a human spirit and soul.

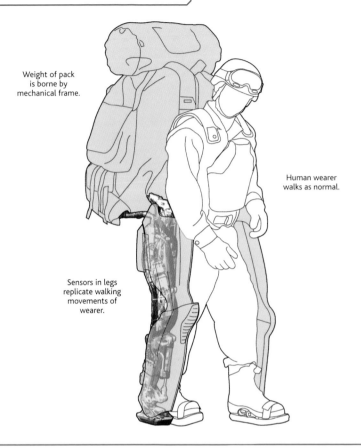

Weight of pack
is borne by
mechanical frame.

Human wearer
walks as normal.

Sensors in legs
replicate walking
movements of
wearer.

The easiest way to understand how BLEEX works is to think of a parent walking with a child standing on his or her feet. The child is responsible for his or her own balance but the parent provides the infrastructure to carry a heavy load.

- The BLEEX exoskeleton connects leg braces made of carbon fibre and plastic to the wearer's modified boots using metal clamps.

- The load-bearing backpack hangs off the pilot's shoulders and is also strapped across his chest.

- Straps can also be used below the knees, although they're optional.

- Over 40 hydraulic actuators and sensors form a local area network, or an artificial nervous system. This provides the system's computer with movement information so it can monitor and adjust a load of up to 32 kilograms (70 pounds).

- The computer runs on an electrical power generated by a 2-horsepower petrol motor, which also powers the hydraulic system. A litre of petrol provides 15 minutes of walking in the prototype. However, BLEEX 2 may be powered with a gas-hybrid engine.

- The exoskeleton itself weighs 45 kilograms (100 pounds), a shortcoming that its inventors are trying to ameliorate in the next generation.

# COMMUNICATIONS ⸫

Remember the distinctive triple chirp of a *Star Trek* communicator? Cordless calls on the go were once strictly the province of science fiction but now we take the technology for granted and have a lifeline wherever we travel – a rare and welcome case of the world of today catching up with the promised world of tomorrow. But where are the telemechanics that allow us to control machines with our thoughts? Where's that hypnopaedia so that we can learn while we sleep? Never mind MTV, we want RTV where the R stands for *retina*: programming on demand projected directly onto your eye.

Technophobes beware: we are rapidly advancing toward a data-on-demand future where countless terabytes will be sent and received continuously, no matter where you are. But some of us will be reaching information nirvana sooner than others: citizens of wealthy nations get the shakes when deprived of their mobile phone wireless Internet access, their Bluetooth PDAs, or their BlackBerrys, while 75 per cent of Africans will never use a phone. Hopefully, the future will see us working toward greater parity where all human beings are interconnected. After all, communication is the key to our understanding of one another. How else will we be able to bridge the divide?

◀ The iconic communications
badge from *Star Trek: The
Next Generation*.

10:12    01-

# COMMUNICATORS
# AND MOBILE PHONES

*Wireless communication systems and mobile handsets allow you to call anyone you like, from wherever you are in the world. You won't ever miss that vital call again – but you also won't be able to use the excuse that you're away from your desk or out of the office if you're trying to avoid an awkward work call.*

## ⠂ SCIENTIFIC HISTORY

⠂ Cellular phone networks were conceived in 1947 at the AT&T Bell Labs but the world's first consumer network wasn't launched until 1971 in Finland. Competing networks started to appear in the United States in the early 1980s. Since then we have seen the emergence of digital networks that allow for more efficient use of the radio spectrum – a necessity as cellular technology became a mass-market phenomenon in the 1990s. The data-enabled phones of the late 1990s were replaced by 3G technology in the early 2000s, allowing wireless access to multimedia content such as games and ringtones.

## ⠂ SIGHTINGS IN SCI-FI

- In his 1946 comic strip, Dick Tracy had a two-way, voice-activated videophone that fitted around his wrist like a watch.

- The portable or mobile phone was predicted in the late 1940s, in Robert Heinlein's short story *Space Cadet*. In his 1953 novel *Assignment in Eternity*, he officially names his device a 'pocketphone'.

- For most of us, though, the first suggestion of the high-tech future of the phone was the *Star Trek* communicator (complete with a flip-up top that was a precursor of modern mobile phone design), which allowed the crew members to talk to each other as well as to other spaceships in orbit.

## ⫶ REALITY

⫶ Mobile phones have substantially surpassed science fiction's original vision. Today you can call anyone in the world using a mobile handset from pretty much any location. While cellular coverage is mostly centred in populated areas, satellite phones can be used to call from the remotest places on the planet, pole to pole.

Voice communication is only one of myriad technologies available on your mobile phone. A new generation of mobile devices, called 'smartphones', gives users handheld wireless computers, complete with digital cameras and will evolve over the next decade to include mobile translators and electronic book readers with high-resolution foldable screens, as well as entertainment storage devices that can show movies and television programmes. They are also likely to have electronic wallet features that will replace credit cards and even take the place of traditional identification cards.

Next-generation data networks, or 4G, will be available by 2010 and will allow for a data transfer speed of up to 1 Gb/s, which would mean you could download an entire *Star Trek* episode in about a minute.

▲ Modern flip-top phones bear a striking resemblance to the original *Star Trek* communicator.

## ⫶ TECH SPEC: WIMAX

A new wireless Internet service called WiMAX (Worldwide Interoperability for Microwave Access) is being considered as the cornerstone of 4G cellular technology. WiMAX was originally designed to bring wireless Internet to areas where a wired infrastructure is not available, such as rural areas or developing countries, but proponents of 4G are now considering it for super-fast mobile data transfer to mobile phones and other mobile computers.

WiMAX is used today to deliver wireless Internet to a fixed receiver, such as the one in your home:

• First you need a WiMAX tower, similar in concept to a mobile phone mast. It is placed at the centre of the coverage area, which can be as large as 7,700 square kilometres (3,000 square miles); in comparison, New York City is packed into a little more than 777 square kilometres (300 square miles).

• The end user has an antenna or dish that can receive the WiMAX signals in two modes:

 • If the WiMAX receiver has line of sight to the tower, it can receive fast Internet service at a frequency of 10–66 GHz

 • Non-line-of-sight service is also available. It uses the 2–11 GHz radio spectrum and can work despite obstructions but has a limited range of 6.5–9.6 kilometres (4–6 miles) or 65 square kilometres (25 square miles) of coverage, similar to a mobile phone mast.

A WiMAX network is capable of delivering 70 Mb/s of service, which is 70 times faster than average home-wired broadband Internet services. However, that bandwidth would be shared among customers, giving them a 1 Mb connection each.

# VIDEOPHONES ⸪

*Even Alexander Graham Bell wanted to see the person he was calling face to face: his first words on the telephone were 'Mr Watson, come here'. Videophones may allow grandparents to watch their faraway grandchildren grow up but the gadgets are also about being nosy – wanting to see a friend's new dress as she leaves the shop or find out if one's partner really is working late . . .*

## ⸬ SCIENTIFIC HISTORY

⸬ The Picturephone, the first working videophone, emerged in 1956 from American telecoms firm Bell Laboratories but could transmit only one image every two seconds. An updated version underwent trials in 1964 and videocall centres were soon set up in New York, Chicago, and Washington, DC; by this time, the picture – around 12.7 centimetres (5 inches) square – was transmitted 30

**1956_**

Bell Laboratories unveil Picturephone

## ⸬ SIGHTINGS IN SCI-FI

- In 1889 Jules Verne, trying to imagine what the world 1,000 years in the future might look like, first mentions what we now call a videophone in his book *In the Year 2889*, calling it the 'phonotelephote'.

- In *Star Trek*, while communicators work for local calls between crewmates, long-distance calls, such as between Star Fleet and the ship, or between family members and the ship's crew, are done via videophone.

- Stanley Kubrick's 1968 movie of Arthur C Clarke's *2001: A Space Odyssey* features a videophone call that Dr Heywood Floyd makes on a public hands-free videophone device that takes a credit card, while William Gibson, in his novel *Count Zero* (1986), describes a phone screen which can be folded away when not in use.

- Pee-Wee Herman used a made-up 'picturephone' in *Pee-Wee's Playhouse* (1986) but real prototypes of the AT&T VideoPhone 2500 could be seen in the movie *Gremlins 2* (1990).

times per second. The first full commercial service began in Pittsburgh in 1970 and the firm predicted a million users by the end of the decade. However, the reality fell rather short and a survey by Bell found that people actually didn't like seeing who they were talking to. A British colour videophone called the BT Relate 2000 was introduced in the 1990s but customers didn't take to that either: it was expensive and the image quality was poor.

## ᐳ REALITY

ᐳ Recently, miniaturisation has enabled mobile phone manufacturers to cram more inside their handsets. The most obvious add-on has been the camera, with new handsets often having two – one for still images and one for video. Mobile videocalling has been made possible by larger bandwidth – the amount of data that can be transmitted in a given time – of third-generation (3G) mobile phone networks. Internet telephony is also being adapted for video, although the quality has yet to match that achieved by 3G videocalling. Videocalls can be pricey but free video instant messaging – where you and your friends use webcams to see each other on your computer screens – might encourage greater uptake.

**1996_**
British Telecom introduce the BT Relate 2000

**1970_**
First commercial videocall service set up in Pittsburgh

**1964_**
Videocall between Disneyland and World's Fair in New York

## ᐳ TECH SPEC: VIDEO CALLS

- A video call consists of two parts: a stream of video images and the accompanying voice. Ever since videophones were first conceived, one of the big challenges has been to get the two parts synchronized; this goes for TV, too. If the components are not accurately synchronised, the difference starts to bother people – humans tend to notice delays of more than about 80 milliseconds.

- Timing pulses and timestamps are used to keep the two locked together: when the audio and video channels are compressed for transmission, each packet of information is labelled with the time according to a very accurate and stable system clock. When the transmission arrives, the receiver examines these 'timestamps' to make sure the video and audio are synchronised.

- The other big challenge is the different amount of bandwidth required for audio and video: for a frame of video, Bell's Picturephone required over 300 times the amount of data needed for the corresponding audio. These days, videophone systems use data compression techniques on the video to enable higher quality pictures to be transmitted over the same bandwidth.

- 3G phones typically use an international compression standard called MPEG-4, developed by the Moving Picture Experts Group in 1999. Although this improves picture quality, it can cause other problems, particularly with timing. Compressing a video signal takes time and the audio signal, which usually takes less time to process, has to be delayed to keep it synchronised.

# EYEPHONES ◁

*Why not avoid expensive and bulky equipment like TV displays and have images projected directly onto your retina instead? With a pair of eyephones disguised as spectacles, not only will you be able to see an image as if it were displayed on a screen as big as a house, you'll be able to project all sorts of useful images about the real world – personal satellite navigation, for example, or facial recognition software so you can call up everything you ever knew about the person you've just bumped into.*

## ⊳ SCIENTIFIC HISTORY

⊳ In 1985, partially sighted poet Elizabeth Goldring was having her eyes tested with a scanning laser ophthalmoscope (SLO) by the machine's inventor, Dr Robert Webb. The extent of a person's blindness is hard to gauge from their own descriptions of what they can and can't see but the SLO gets around this by shining a thin laser beam onto the retina and measuring the reflected light.

Although the SLO was designed for diagnosis, Goldring recognised the device's potential as a way for visually impaired people to see objects and began developing it further with Dr Webb and researchers at the Schepens Eye Research Institute in Boston.

Further research into retinal projection took place at the Human Interface Technology Laboratory of the University of Washington in Seattle a few years later. The virtual retinal display (VRD) was conceived there in 1991 and prototypes were built by Dr Thomas A Furness, Joel Kollin and Bob Burstein two years later. Early prototypes used a red laser and a complicated series of optics to project a beam directly onto the retina. However, these could only produce single-colour, low-resolution images, were hard to align with the eye, and were very costly.

Other prototypes followed, including one that could produce images in full colour by combining light from red, green, and blue

> **1985_**
>
> First research into use of lasers to combat sight problems

◀ The human eye uses light reflected from objects to build up a picture of the world around us.

lasers, albeit at huge cost and at the expense of portability. A briefcase-sized portable system that works in a single colour has also been developed.

## ⋗ REALITY

⋗ In spring 2006, Elizabeth Goldring and her colleagues at MIT's Center for Advanced Visual Studies unveiled the Retinal Imaging Machine Visual System, or RIMVS for short. The machine enabled a group of visually impaired subjects to read words and see simple images that were projected directly onto their retinas.

The RIMVS is a development of the laser-powered SLO, and replaces the laser element with a series of light-emitting diodes (LEDs) that project directly into the pupil. This change has meant that the new system can be built for just a few thousand US dollars instead of the US$100,000 required to build an SLO, and that a wider variety of colours of light can be projected without the need for a mass of extra equipment.

As well as aiding the visually impaired, the potential uses for an eyephone, combined with virtual reality, are amazingly diverse. They might range from a clock overlaid onto your vision, to totally immersive simulations for trainee pilots or surgeons of complicated landing procedures or medical operations. They could give soldiers a map of their location and surrounding terrain at the blink of an eye or be used for one-person cinema screenings to keep us occupied on long-haul flights without disturbing other passengers.

### 2006_
Retinal Imaging Machine Visual System unveiled

### 1993_
First VRD prototypes built

### 1991_
Virtual Retinal Display (VRD) first conceived

---

## ⋗ SIGHTINGS IN SCI-FI

- In the 1952 novel *The Space Merchants*, authors Frederik Pohl and C M Kornbluth came up with the theory that instead of having to view a screen, you could project an image directly onto the retina. We get a sneak preview of the possible result in the 1984 movie *The Terminator* (right), where the cyborg's view of the world is overlaid with targeting information.

- The projection of images directly onto the retina is now a cyberpunk tradition and the nifty devices appear under different titles in various films and novels – retinal projectors are called 'Eyephones' in William Gibson's 1996 novel *Idoru* and 'Eyecaps' in the 1999 novel *Starfish* by Peter Watts.

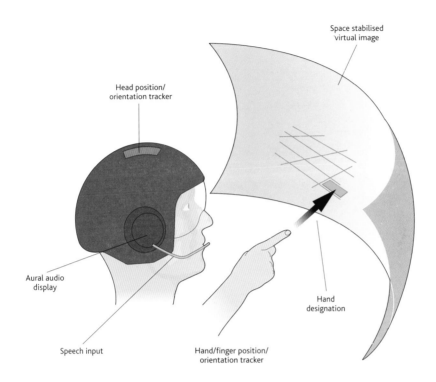

Space stabilised virtual image

Head position/ orientation tracker

Aural audio display

Speech input

Hand/finger position/ orientation tracker

Hand designation

Before considering how an eyephone would work, it is worth thinking back to school and how the human eye works. When you look at an object, light reflected from its surface enters your eye and is focused through the lens onto your retina, a thin layer of nerve cells that covers the back of the eyeball. When you watch television, there is a subtle difference: instead of reflected light, you see light that has been projected onto the inside of the television screen.

With an eyephone, instead of viewing an image on screen, an image is projected directly into the eye using a laser beam, effectively faking what you would experience if you were viewing a scene directly:

- Lasers build up an image incrementally in a series of lines, in the same way that a television image is produced.

- The intensity of the beam varies as it scans across each line to build up the image.

- Lasers emit light at a very specific frequency. This means that the colour is purer than with white light, which is made up of light of different frequencies/colours, so lasers produce a much sharper image.

The result may spell the end for bulky visual equipment.

# ELECTRONIC BOOKS AND PAPER ⁝

*The books of the future won't be made of vast reams of paper and you won't need a library to house your collection. Instead, you'll be able to read books on a handheld computer and store your favourite novels digitally. Electronic paper and ink will allow for a portable display that looks like a book and feels like a book but has dozens of books, newspapers or magazines in its memory.*

## ⁝ SCIENTIFIC HISTORY

⁝ Today's electronic books have their roots in 'talking books' – voice recordings on vinyl records that were first available in 1933 and which were originally developed for the blind. However, the 'e-book' (a book that you can download from the Internet) wasn't invented until 1971; since then creator Michael Hart has been working on Project Gutenberg, putting thousands of books into electronic format and making them available for download.

### 1960_

Books on tape available in the US Library of Congress

## ⁝ SIGHTINGS IN SCI-FI

• Electronic books and paper are relatively recent innovations in the world of sci-fi. In Stanislav Lem's 1961 novel *Return from the Stars*, the narrator misses paper books, since the 'books' of his day are crystals that are read electronically. The handheld electronic book that we know today was predicted in 1979 in Douglas Adams' *The Hitchhiker's Guide to the Galaxy*.

• In Stephen Spielberg's 2002 movie *Minority Report*, Tom Cruise, playing John Anderton, is shown reading an electronic newspaper: a sheet of paper-thin plastic film written over with electronically manipulated ink. An earlier reference to this kind of technology was made in Neal Stephenson's 1995 novel *The Diamond Age*.

The father of electronic paper, however, is Nick Sheridon, who, while working at Xerox in the early 1970s, invented Gyricon. This first electronic paper used electricity to rotate microscopic black and white balls on a sheet of rubber to create pixels.

Printing and publishing companies continued to develop electronic ink and paper technologies in the 2000s. In 2006, Belgian newspaper *De Tijd* began selling an electronic version of their publication, to be displayed on an E-Ink device. The newspaper can be connected to the Internet and updated daily.

## ⪢ REALITY

⪢ Books that can be displayed on a computer have been around for three decades. However, they have yet to challenge the dominance of paper books, primarily because publishers have instituted copy protections, making them more difficult to use and less convenient than paper books. In addition, an expensive computing device that requires battery power is needed to display them and these tend to be less comfortable and easy to read than paper books.

The situation may change with the introduction of a new generation of high-resolution, low-powered electronic paper devices that began to appear commercially in 2006, with the release of the Sony Reader and the competing iLiad from iRex Technologies. The tablets, which use E-Ink technology, can display books, magazines and newspapers.

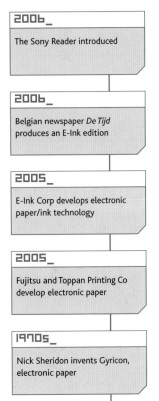

**2006_**
The Sony Reader introduced

**2006_**
Belgian newspaper *De Tijd* produces an E-Ink edition

**2005_**
E-Ink Corp develops electronic paper/ink technology

**2005_**
Fujitsu and Toppan Printing Co develop electronic paper

**1970S_**
Nick Sheridon invents Gyricon, electronic paper

## ⪢ TECH SPEC: ILIAD ELECTRONIC PAPER

Perhaps the most successful commercialised electronic book technology was created by E-Ink Corp, which is used in the iLiad from iRex Technologies. Here's how it works:

- Millions of tiny microcapsules, the width of a human hair, are filled with a clear liquid.

- Tiny black and white particles float in the liquid: the white ones are positively charged and the black ones are negatively charged.

- When a negatively charged electrical field is generated, the white particles float to the top of the microcapsule and the black ones sink, so the microcapsule appears white.

- When a positive field is generated the black particles float and the capsule appears black.

- Each capsule represents a pixel or dot of black. By manipulating the electrical field, pixels can be created or erased, allowing for complex images and type to be displayed at a resolution of about 170 pixels per inch (2.5 centimetres).

# LANGUAGE TRANSLATORS ⋖

*Never again will you have to worry about learning a foreign language or remembering the correct foreign phrase at a key moment. Simply speak into a handheld device and have it translate your words perfectly into any one of 6,000 languages; your interlocuter's words are then translated back into English for you.*

## ⋗ SCIENTIFIC HISTORY

⋗ Bell Laboratories demonstrated the Voder, the first electronic speech synthesiser, at the 1939 World's Fair. By the 1980s, voice recognition software was developed for desktop computers; translation software appeared in 1986 with Diplomat, a sort of electronic dictionary.

In 2001, US soldiers in Afghanistan used the Phraselator P2 to communicate with local people; and in 2004, Japanese company NEC launched the first handheld translating device, which recognises spoken words in one language and translates them to another, playing back the translation with a voice synthesiser.

## ⋗ SIGHTINGS IN SCI-FI

- The makers of television shows *Stargate SG-1* and *Stargate Atlantis* made the decision that all characters, both alien and human, would speak English in order to save spending ten minutes an episode on characters learning a new language. But language translators do occur elsewhere in sci-fi.

- In *Doctor Who*, the TARDIS automatically translates all languages into a language understood by the reader or listener; *Star Trek* uses the Universal Translator; and in Douglas Adams' novel, *The Hitchhiker's Guide to the Galaxy*, space travellers can drop a Babel fish into their ear and instantly be able to understand any language in the universe.

◀ The Phraselator P2 is the automatic translator of choice for the US Army.

## ⁑ REALITY

⁑ Hand-held translators exist today but they are limited to single phrases or words rather than continuous speech. However, SRI International, an independent research institute, has designed a two-way, voice-activated system that can translate between English and Iraqi Arabic using a laptop PC. The DARPA-funded project has a vocabulary of 40,000 English and 50,000 Iraqi Arabic words.

More advanced translators, like those on *Star Trek*, however, remain elusive – programming a computer to recognise a known language is one thing, programming it to decode a completely new language is quite another.

## ⁑ TECH SPEC: PHRASELATOR

The Phraselator P2, a translation system funded by DARPA (the Defense Advanced Research Projects Agency, the central research and development organisation for the US Department of Defense), is a one-way translator that can be used to speak phrases in a foreign language. The user can download phrases in up to 45 languages from the Internet. Speciality modules for law enforcement and military use are also available.

The user can access phrases in three ways:

- Scrolling through an on-screen menu and selecting one with a button click
- Tapping the device with a stylus
- Speaking an English phrase

The translated phrase is then played back from an MP3 audio file originally recorded by a human speaker.

The device can also be used to record responses for later translation by a human. Cleverly, the phrases are designed so that they can elicit a response using nonverbal communication such as a nod of the head or a gesture. So, for example, a user could say to someone who had been injured, 'Show me where it hurts'. The victim could then respond by pointing to the relevant area.

# HYPNOPAEDIA :·

*Sleep learning is every student's dream – waking up with the facts you need for tomorrow's exam would save hours of studying. If only it existed.*

## ::· SCIENTIFIC HISTORY

::· The idea of using otherwise wasted sleep time for learning originates in the late 19th century, when the phonograph was developed, and Sigmund Freud proposed the idea of a subconscious sleeping mind with the power to record and process data.

Studies throughout the 1940s and 1950s suggested that sleep learning did have some effect. In 1942, one study concluded that hypnopaedia was successful in discouraging a group of boys at summer camp from biting their nails, while in 1952, another study showed it was possible to teach Chinese to people while they were asleep.

Further research in the 1950s, however, suggested that sleep learning takes place when sleepers are partially woken, although they don't recall this sleep disturbance once they are awake. Since

### ::· SIGHTINGS IN SCI-FI

- Sleep learning first appeared in Hugo Gernsback's 1911 short story 'Ralph 124c 41 +', published in *Modern Electrics*.

- The idea firmly took root in Aldous Huxley's dystopian 1932 novel *Brave New World* in which hypnopaedia is used to indoctrinate children.

- Lately, the idea of sleep learning has been surpassed by the virtual reality education of *The Matrix* (1999), where Neo learns kung fu in minutes by downloading the skills directly to his brain.

◀ The theory of hypnopaedia is that the unconscious sleeping mind can take in and remember repeated messages.

then hypnopaedia has been largely disregarded, as no conclusive research has yet been produced to suggest it is efficient or particularly effective as a learning tool.

## ⫶ REALITY

⫶ Scientists have their doubts about the efficacy of hynopaedia, though there is some evidence that learning in your sleep may reinforce learning during the daytime. This discovery, a result of a series of Russian studies in the 1960s, led one group to recommend that hypnopaedia be used to assist secondary school students in their lessons. However, the discovery that knowledge could only be taken in if sleep patterns were disturbed leads many scientists to conclude that a good night's sleep followed by an hour's conscious learning is probably more effective.

For those interested in napping their way to knowledge, pillow speakers and learning CDs are available today.

## ⫶ TECH SPEC: SLEEP LEARNING

- Studies suggest that repetitive audio messages played while you sleep, over a series of successive nights, may help you retain new information.

- The consensus appears to be that learning occurs during brief disruptions to the sleep pattern, which researchers term 'microarousals'.

# VIRTUAL
# CONFERENCING ⫶

*In the future, when our carbon dioxide emissions mean we must pay sky-high taxes, we may think twice about travelling for a face-to-face meeting and simply have virtual conferences instead. High-definition cameras and plasma screens have made virtual meetings with colleagues real: they look and sound as though they are sitting just a few feet away. And fully 3D, holographic conferencing isn't far away.*

## ⫶ SCIENTIFIC HISTORY

⫶ Using early television, Germany developed a rudimentary video conferencing system in the late 1930s, but the Second World War prevented further development. The first steps toward virtual conferencing were taken in 1968 at Douglas Engelbart's exposition of the first computer mouse, examples of hypertext and bitmapped screens. There was also a real-time (audiovisual) video conference, whose participants collaborated on a shared document.

Making video conferencing seem real requires both bandwidth and video compression techniques in order to transmit images in

**1930S_**

Germany develops basic video conferencing

## ⫶ SIGHTINGS IN SCI-FI

- George Orwell's *1984* (written in 1948) introduced the 'telescreen', by which Big Brother could both communicate with and spy on the inhabitants of the state Airstrip One.

- For years on *Star Trek* we saw long-distance meetings and conferences on flat screens, which

became a standard sci-fi convention and a precursor to modern Internet webcams.

- It was the cyberpunk era, however, starting with William Gibson's *Neuromancer* in 1984, that gave us the idea that people could connect and interact in virtual space.

real time. In 1984, the first digital coding standard, H.120, was released by the standardising body CCITT, paving the way for smoother transmission of video. ISDN (Integrated Services Digital Network) telephone services followed in 1987, increasing the bandwidth available for voice and data transmisson over telephone wires. Video conferencing systems appeared in the 1990s but it was another decade before virtual conferencing appeared.

## ⁑ REALITY

⁑ The new generation of virtual conferencing is in use as we speak. Hewlett Packard, with movie company Dreamworks, launched the Halo program in 2005 and Cisco has recently launched a competing system called TelePresence.

The key to the Halo system is specially designed conference rooms that are identical, down to the fabric and lighting. Each room contains half of a round conference table, with the other half appearing virtually on the screen. High-resolution cameras and flat screens show the meeting participants in remote locations at life size, and the identical décor tricks the eye into seeing the screen as part of the same room. There are currently public rooms in 12 locations worldwide, including New York, London and Singapore. The technology is not cheap, however: a Halo room costs half a million dollars to install, while network and service fees currently cost US$18,000 a month.

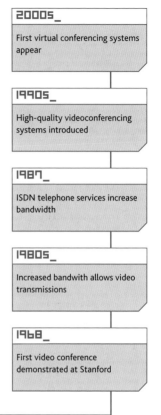

**2000s_**
First virtual conferencing systems appear

**1990s_**
High-quality videoconferencing systems introduced

**1987_**
ISDN telephone services increase bandwidth

**1980s_**
Increased bandwith allows video transmissions

**1968_**
First video conference demonstrated at Stanford

## ⁑ TECH SPEC: HP HALO

The HP Halo setup requires a bandwidth of 45 megabits per second, equivalent to sending the full text of the Bible every second. Even with this high bandwidth, some compression of the audio and video is required. Halo uses a compression standard called MPEG-2. This takes advantage of the fact that consecutive frames of video are often very similar, particularly in video conferencing, where the meeting participants are often sitting still and only moving their mouths.

• Each image is broken down into small blocks.

• These blocks are compared with blocks in the previous image to find those that appear similar – for example, a part of the image containing a meeting participant's earring.

• Encoding small differences such as how this block has moved between the two consecutive images usually takes up considerably less bandwidth than encoding every pixel of each image.

• As a result, a compressed video feed might need to encode a full image only every 15 frames.

# WATCH GADGETS ⋮

*When the digital watch burst onto the scene after centuries of relative quiet in the world of watches, manufacturers realised that the timepiece on your arm could do much more than tell time. The watch has the potential to become the convergence device for all our gadgets. Imagine having a watch that could record high-quality video clips, phone your friends, let you surf the net, act as an electronic purse and monitor your health, all while keeping time.*

## ⋮ SCIENTIFIC HISTORY

⋮ Just under 500 years ago, German locksmith Peter Henlein invented the Nuremberg egg, the first portable clock or watch. Since then, watchmakers have vied to add new features to their wristwatches. Rolex came up with automatic dates and the first watches with dual time zones. The Bulgarian NASA engineer Peter Petroff, with John Bergey and Richard Walton from Hamilton Military Products, developed the first digital watches in the late 1960s and early 1970s. In 1982 Japanese watchmakers Seiko wowed the world with their 'TV Watch'. The watch face featured an LCD screen measuring 2.5 centimetres wide by 1.7 centimetres high (1 by ²/₃ inches) on which you could watch television for up to five hours on two ordinary AA batteries. Because the display did not have backlighting, it was difficult to watch in bright light. The designers cheated a little; you had to carry around a separate pack containing the tuner and batteries.

A year later, Seiko took a leap toward wearable computing with the launch of the Data-2000. It was the size of a typical digital watch but it came with a separate keyboard. Communication between the two was achieved by placing the watch on the keyboard's 'transmission circuit' and pressing the watch's transmit button.

> **1524_**
>
> Peter Henlein invents the first portable clock

◀ Gone are the days when all a watch could do was tell you the time.

**1983_**

Seiko releases the Data-2000 watch

**1982_**

Seiko unveils the TV Watch

**1960s_**

The first digital watches appear

The first true wrist computer didn't appear until the year 2000. Fossil released its Wrist PDA in 2002; it was little bigger than a standard watch but packed in the functionality of a personal digital assistant. Running on the Palm operating system, better known for larger devices like the PalmPilot and the Treo, the Wrist PDA had a 160 by 160 mono screen, 2 MB of memory and offered applications such as an address book, a calculator and a to-do list.

## ⁞ SIGHTINGS IN SCI-FI

It was, of course, the James Bond books and films that gave us the most exciting selection of watch gadgets:

- In the early 1960s, Bond had a watch that glowed in the dark; his enemies had a watch from which a thin wire could be pulled and used to strangle someone.

- By the 1970s Bond had upgraded to a magnetic watch, which could deflect a bullet with its attraction, and also had a 'pager' watch that allowed him to receive messages from HQ.

- Bond's watch in the 1980s contained everything needed to make an instant bomb, including a remote detonator. A built-in two-way radio and digital messaging capabilities allowed Bond to remain in contact on the move.

- By the 1990s and beyond, Bond's watch had a built-in laser cutter, more explosives and a remote detonator – and even a grappling hook with 15 metres (50 feet) of strong microfilament.

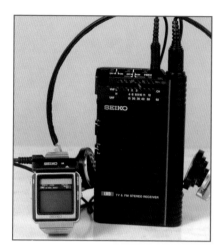

◄ The Seiko TV watch was released in 1982, heralding a new era in gadgets.

**2002_**

Fossil release Wrist PDA, the first true wrist computer

## ⸬ REALITY

⸬ Finnish firm Suunto has dispensed with the concept of 'the watch' altogether, instead styling their products 'wrist-top computers'. These gadgets do still tell the time but various models can also tell you how deep you are diving, how fast you are skiing, how fast your heart is beating and how good your backswing was. Many of the firm's watches incorporate GPS technology to pinpoint your position anywhere on the globe, a testament to how far miniaturisation of electronics has developed. A New Zealand company called Rakon has announced that its latest GPS receiver will be the size of a baby's fingernail – which would leave plenty of space in a watch for other exciting stuff. In 2006, Seiko introduced a Bluetooth-enabled watch that could communicate with its owner's mobile phone to announce incoming calls or new text messages.

A recent survey found that people are increasingly relying on their mobile phones to tell the time and the watch may be in danger of becoming sidelined. Watchmakers have therefore had to up the ante and even the presentation of time on watches has become an area of innovation, with bizarre watch displays popping up all over the place. At the forefront of this time tinkering is Japanese fashion watch firm Tokyo Flash. The firm's Equalizer watch has echoes of the graphic equaliser on your hi-fi, with green bars flashing away until only a few dots are left to show the time.

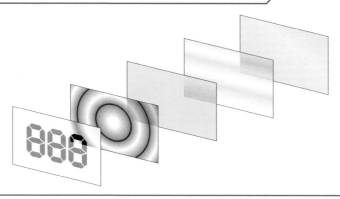

Miniaturisation has been the key to expanding the humble watch beyond basic time telling, and it was the invention of the integrated circuit in the late 1950s and the microprocessor in the late 1960s and early 1970s that really spurred watchmakers into doing things other than mere timekeeping.

The invention of the quartz-controlled watch in 1969 also played its part. At the heart of many modern watches is a small bar of quartz crystal. Quartz exhibits a property known as piezoelectricity, which means that it vibrates at a specific frequency when a voltage is applied to it, typically 32,768 hertz. This number is significant – it is 2 to the power of 15, or 2 multiplied by itself 15 times. The quartz signal is then fed several times through a circuit that halves the frequency of any input applied to it, eventually reducing the signal to 1 hertz. By happy coincidence, a signal with a frequency of 1 hertz (meaning it repeats itself once per second) is just what we need to count off the seconds on a watch.

Advances in display technology have also helped the development of watch gadgets. Early digital watches used light-emitting diode (LED) technology. LEDs are essentially semiconductor compounds, such as gallium arsenide, which emit a specific colour of light when a voltage is applied to them. However, LED technology was rapidly superseded by the liquid crystal display (LCD), which can be run on less power.

- LCDs are sandwiches consisting of two outer transparent electrodes, two polarising filters within those, and a central layer of liquid crystal between the filters.

- Backlit LCDs have a light to the rear of this sandwich, while those without backlighting have a rear layer that reflects ambient light.

- When no voltage is applied between the electrodes, light (from the backlight or the ambient light) passes through the display unaffected.

- The direction of vibration of a light wave as it travels is known as its polarisation: the wave might be vibrating up and down or left to right, for instance. A polarising filter only allows through light that is vibrating in one particular direction. An LCD uses a pair of polarising filters with their permitted directions at right angles to each other. This means that normally no light passes through. However, the liquid crystal is sandwiched between two filters. When a voltage is applied to the crystal, the wave is twisted as it passes through, allowing light to pass through both filters and be seen on the other side.

- A watch display might be made up of thousands of these filter sandwiches and a voltage can be applied to each one of these sandwiches individually. If the sandwiches are small enough, the pattern of light and dark can be used to make up an image, allowing watchmakers to turn watches into mini-computers.

# WIRELESS ACCESS POINTS ∵

*In the past, if a group of friends in a bar started reminiscing about Spider-Man and tried to remember the words from the theme tune, everyone would have thought for a moment or two and then said, 'No, it's gone'. Now you can tap 'Spider-Man theme' into the Web on your PDA, connect to the bar's wireless access point and get the answer. As wireless Internet spreads to the remotest parts of the globe, you'll never need to remember another piece of trivia again.*

## ∵ SCIENTIFIC HISTORY

∵ Wireless networks began with the invention of radio at the end of the 19th century. Wireless telegraphy appeared during the First World War and was used to transmit encrypted Morse Code signals.

The first true wireless data network, called ALOHNet, appeared in Hawaii in 1971 and connected seven computers on four islands by radio. The need for wireless access to networks was underlined in 1981 when the first laptop computer, the Osborne 1, was publicly released. However, use of wireless networks didn't become widespread until 1990, with the establishment of a new working group of America's Institute of Electrical and Electronics Engineers (IEEE). Working group 11, focusing on local wireless area networks, was part of a committee, numbered 802, specialising in localised computer networks. It took until 1997 for wireless devices using the group's standards to start appearing. The devices were limited in number and it took another year or two – and the release of the 802.11b standard – for wireless Internet, or Wi-Fi, to really take off. The portion of the radio network used by 802.11b is unlicensed in many countries, including the United States, so it is very easy to set

> **1971_**
>
> First wireless network service created in Hawaii

◀ The wireless revolution really began in 2003 when Intel's Centrino program meant wireless technology in laptops was the norm.

**1990_**

Working group 802.11 set up

**1981_**

First laptop computers available to general public

up a wireless network. Sales of wireless access points, wireless routers and slim wireless cards took off. The wireless revolution was boosted in 2003 when Intel launched Centrino, putting wireless technology inside laptops.

## ⸖ REALITY

⸖ Most new laptops, as well as devices such as PDAs and Sony's PSP handheld games console, now have Wi-Fi capability as standard. Sales of laptops are also closing in on those of desktop computers, making wireless Internet access around the home and the office

## ⸖ SIGHTINGS IN SCI-FI

- Murray Leinster may well be the theoretical father of the Internet because of his 1946 short story *A Logic Named Joe*. In it, people use something called a logic – which is actually a lot like a modern-day PC – to watch TV, get news and weather information, send mail, play games and even trade stocks.

- While the Internet became more important in the cyberpunk novels of the 1980s, even recent films

such as *The Matrix* trilogy required people to use a physical interface or 'jack' to connect to a computer network. The idea of ubiquitous Internet wireless access points, where you simply need a modem or a modem card to connect to the Internet or any large network, was missed by the majority of science fiction creators, who simply didn't see it coming . . .

◄ Real-life trials of WiMAX mean individual hotspots may eventually be linked into hotzones and in turn into 'hotstates' and 'hotcountries'.

**1997_**

Wireless devices using 802.11 standard appear

**1999_**

802.11b standard released; Wi-Fi takes off

**2003_**

Intel Centrino puts Wi-Fi technology into laptops

much more in demand. Over the past few years, Internet service providers have set up wireless access points worldwide in key locations such as hotels, airports, railway stations, coffee shops and even burger joints. These can be free to use or require a password that can be purchased on a one-time or subscription basis. At the beginning of 2006, there were estimated to be more than 100,000 hotspots worldwide and the number is increasing day by day.

But some people want full access to online multiplayer games with amazing graphics, while simultaneously downloading a 10 MB presentation, uploading a 20 MB video clip to their blog and using Internet telephony. As a result, in some towns and cities around the world, service providers have installed a number of wirelessly linked access points around a large area to create a 'hotzone' of blanket wireless coverage. Philadelphia is making wireless Internet available throughout the whole city and has pilot areas in the historic square mile. In London, The Cloud has created hotzones in Canary Wharf and The City.

WiMAX (Worldwide Interoperability for Microwave Access) seems likely to be the next big step in wireless technology. This system, again developed by the IEEE, is set to extend the range over which wireless works by many miles and promises a huge increase in the speed of data transmisson. WiMAX is considered a 'last-mile' technology in that it will enable wireless Internet service providers to provide broadband to their customers wherever they may be.

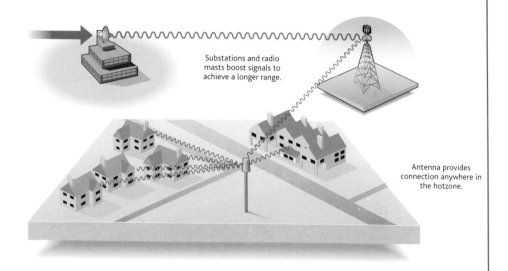

Substations and radio masts boost signals to achieve a longer range.

Antenna provides connection anywhere in the hotzone.

- A basic wireless network has just two elements: a wireless access point and a wireless-enabled device. Wi-Fi protocols transmit data using radio waves, so both of these devices include miniature antennae that can transmit and receive radio signals. Connect the wireless access point to the telephone line via a modem, and you get wireless Internet.

- The two most common wireless systems in use are 802.11b and 802.11g, both of which use a radio frequency of 2.4 gigahertz. Another system, called 802.11a, uses a radio frequency of around 5 GHz. The choice of frequency was important to the growth of Wi-Fi because in many countries – including the United States – you can make transmissions on this part of the radio spectrum without having to obtain a licence from the government. Cordless phones and devices that use Bluetooth also operate at this frequency and these devices can interfere with each other and cause a degradation of the wireless network.

- Wireless devices working to the 802.11b standard have a maximum theoretical data rate of 11 megabits per second, enough to transmit the information in a typical phonebook in just a few seconds. However, the maximum data rate users can expect is around half of the theoretical maximum and interference from other 2.4 gigahertz transmissions can reduce this further. Theoretically, 802.11b devices have a maximum range of around 100 metres (35 feet) but buildings with thick walls and unfavourable atmospheric conditions can reduce this.

- Some of these problems will be addressed by the latest WiMAX standard, 802.16e, which uses multiple antennae to give a better signal. One of the key differences between Wi-Fi and WiMAX is how data is handled when multiple users are in the same location. With Wi-Fi, the users furthest away from the access point are likely to receive slower access than those closer in. With WiMAX, all users receive equal bandwidth.

# FUTURE INTERNET ‹

*When you look at the incredible variety of services available on the Internet, it's hard to imagine that the original goals of the Internet's pioneers were limited to academic research. Web 2.0, the second generation of the Web, has user-generated content and communities, but Web 3.0 is more interesting: information on the Web will be smart-tagged to automatically create new resources and links.*

## ⁘ SCIENTIFIC HISTORY

⁘ In 1958, President Dwight D Eisenhower set up the Advanced Research Projects Agency (ARPA) within the US Department of Defense in response to the launch of *Sputnik* by the Soviet Union. In the 1960s, ARPA began work on a system called ARPANET, a wide area network of linked computers. The original idea was to link computers at academic and military locations to share resources for defence research. In 1969, a computer at UCLA and another at the Stanford Research Institute were connected. When a user at one logged on remotely to the other, what would eventually become the Internet was born. By 1977 the ARPANET had 100 computers and in 1984 the introduction of domain name servers gave us the now familiar suffixes .com, .gov and so on.

> **1958_**
>
> Eisenhower sets up ARPA

The World Wide Web was the brainchild of Tim Berners-Lee, a British systems developer working at the European Organization for Nuclear Research (CERN) laboratory in Geneva in 1989. Berners-Lee describes the Web as 'an Internet-based hypermedia initiative for global information sharing'. In 1990, he wrote the first Web browser, initially called WorldWideWeb but later rechristened Nexus. The World Wide Web became the standard protocol for transmission of data, which companies or institutions could post to their websites for users anywhere in the world to access.

◀ British systems developer Tim Berners-Lee invented the World Wide Web in 1990.

**1969_**

First two computers linked using ARPANET

**1968_**

ARPA starts work on ARPANET

Technology since then has made access to data faster and cheaper. Private users are no longer limited to downloading data – these days anyone can set up their own Web space to share their own thoughts, photos, videos and music and interact with others. This new, truly interactive Internet is known as Web 2.0.

## ⊳ REALITY

⊳ Web 2.0 is causing no end of buzz. The popularity of user-generated sites – sites on which all data is provided by the community of users – such as YouTube, MySpace, Facebook, Flickr, Wikipedia and

## ⊳ SIGHTINGS IN SCI-FI

- There are very few references to the Internet and the World Wide Web in sci-fi; this is one area where the sci-fi writers, who were visionaries in so many of their predictions, failed big time. No one saw it coming, or saw it moving so fast once it got here.

- In *Star Trek*, the computer is an Internet device with a voice interface, having the Google-like ability to search through massive archives with verbal queries.

- Meanwhile, the 1995 Sandra Bullock thriller, *The Net*, about a computer expert whose identity is tampered with to include a police record because she holds key information, was an early illustration of identity theft – and inadvertently popularised the term 'Net'.

▲ A party in Second Life, a 3D virtual world that offers its residents all manner of entertainment and experiences.

**1977_**

100 computers are connected using ARPANET

**1984_**

First domain names appear

**1999_**

First browser, WorldWideWeb, is created

del.icio.us has broken down the barriers between the providers and the consumers of information: now, anyone can publish a newspaper, run a radio show or create a television station.

Second Life, a three-dimensional virtual world developed by Linden Labs, opened online in 2003 and now has more than eight million inhabitants. Inside Second Life, you can chat with other inhabitants, attend concerts by real-life bands, have virtual sex and trade using virtual currency. Inhabitants have created a thriving economy: millions of 'Linden dollars' change hands every month; there are online exchanges where you can swap Linden dollars for real-life currency. In 2006, Second Life inhabitant Anshe Chung became the first person to achieve a net worth exceeding US$1 million from profits earned entirely inside a virtual world.

Web 3.0 promises even more. Artificial intelligence will manage data organically, linking content across applications independently of the user – search engines will not only classify data but understand its meaning. Your accounts on Flickr and Second Life might be linked so that your photos automatically appear on the walls of your virtual home. Your favourite websites will automatically inform you when they're updated. And a host of new security features will recognise private or sensitive information, and screen incoming and outgoing data to keep your secrets safe.

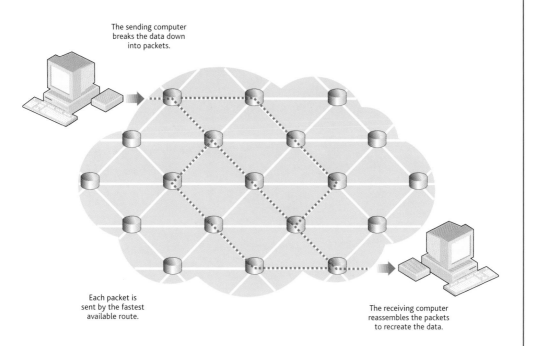

The sending computer breaks the data down into packets.

Each packet is sent by the fastest available route.

The receiving computer reassembles the packets to recreate the data.

The Internet relies on something called packet switching. This was conceived by Paul Baran, of the defence agency RAND, in 1952 to render a communications network resistant to nuclear attack:

- The information to be communicated over a network is broken down into small packets which are labelled with their origin and destination.

- The packet is sent off into the Internet and forwarded between computers until it reaches its final destination.

- Any packets lost on the way, through garbling or the destruction of a cable for example, can be re-sent via another route until all the packets are received.

- Because each packet might take a different route to reach its destination, they may arrive out of sequence but they can be easily put back into the correct order by examining the labels and reordering the packets before sending to the recipient.

- A special device called a router decides on the best route for each packet between parts of the network. The router's memory lists the fastest routes for sending information and which connections lead to other parts of the Internet. When it receives a packet, it looks at the destination information it contains and decides the best way to send it.

# WEAPONS AND SECURITY ∴

The prospect of possessing something new and dangerous speaks to us on a primal level, as if we were cavemen once again first contemplating fire. The question of how best to use the latest destructive force provokes a struggle within us: our inner Darth Vader craving power for the sake of power, against our inner Obi-Wan Kenobi, who knows that power has a price.

Not everyone has an inner Jedi to keep them from the dark side and these people have to be watched – hence the need for security. Technology has progressed to the point where even a small number of dedicated individuals can cause massive harm; this calls for heavy surveillance of those who can't be trusted and novel ways to outwit, outfight or outlast any potential threat.

Scientists suggest that the universe should be teeming with extraterrestrial life but thus far we've found nothing. The loneliness of outer space points to the preciousness and fragility of life here on Earth – maybe the reason we have yet to detect an alien signal is the tendency for civilisations that achieve a certain level of technology to self-destruct. Are we on the same path or can we keep our most dangerous toys in their boxes and build a future for the greater good?

◀ The soldier of the future, as envisioned in the movie *Starship Troopers*.

# RETINAL SCANNING ∷

*Forget fingerprints: retinal scanning is one of the most accurate identification technologies yet known. Soon you can expect to have your eyeball examined when you visit the airport or the bank, to make sure you are whom you claim to be.*

## ⸭ SCIENTIFIC HISTORY

⸭ In 1935, ophthalmologists Carleton Simon and Isadore Goldstein revealed in 'A New Scientific Method of Identification', that the pattern of blood vessels found in the back of the eye was unique to an individual.

Commercial development of retinal-identification technology did not start until the 1970s, when the Belgian firm EyeDentify began building scanners. The first scanners used visible light but the developers found that the light had to be uncomfortably bright to achieve a clear scan. An alternative device using invisible near-infrared light was developed at the beginning of the 1980s, with the first commercial scanner, the EyeDentification System 7.5, appearing in 1985.

## ⸭ SIGHTINGS IN SCI-FI

- The retinal scanner became popular in movies such as *Star Trek II* (1982), where one is used to protect the high-security Genesis project files.

- In the 1983 James Bond movie *Never Say Never Again*, a baddie has an eyeball replaced so he can get control of a nuclear weapon.

- In the more recent *Minority Report* (2002), scanners are everywhere, including public places such as subway stations, allowing the powers that be to track everyone's movements and activities.

As one of the most secure biometric technologies around, retinal eye scanning may soon become commonplace.

## ⫶ REALITY

⫶ Retinal scanning is most commonly in use in high-security situations. In 1990, the sheriff's office in Cook County, Illinois, used scanning to confirm the identity of prisoners due for release. Meanwhile, in Iraq, joining the police force (in Ramadi) or getting an ID card (in Fallujah) requires a retinal scan.

Retinal scans can help in other species as well. Researchers at New Mexico State University use US$3,000 retinal scanners with suction eye cups designed for a cow's face to identify and track cattle that have been exposed to disease.

## ⫶ TECH SPEC: RETINAL SCANNING

The retina is a thin film of nerve cells covering the inside of your eyeball. It is useful for biometric identification because the pattern of blood vessels across the retina is unique to an individual, in the same way that each person's fingerprints are unique.

- The subject puts their eye close to the scanner and looks at a light. This ensures that the eyeball is in the correct position for scanning.

- The scanner shines near-infrared light onto the retina and measures what is reflected back. Near-infrared light is used because the reading can be taken much more quickly than if visible light was used, typically in a few seconds.

- The reflected light is captured on a sensitive charge couple device, the imaging system at the centre of digital cameras, and details of up to 400 reference points are stored in a data file.

- This file is very small, so the scan can quickly be compared against millions of others to find a match.

Proponents of retinal scanning say it is far more accurate than other biometric identification techniques – almost a hundred times more accurate than scanning the iris, another part of the eye, for example.

# BIOCHIPS AND ARTIFICIAL IMPLANTS ∷

*Instead of spending years taking Mandarin lessons or learning to fly a helicopter, simply pop open the USB port on the back of your skull, insert a 1-terabyte pen drive containing the necessary knowledge and download it directly into your brain extension RAM. Want a coffee while you're downloading? Pass your finger over a scanner and the implanted chip sends a signal to your bank account to deduct the cost of a decaf skinny mochaccino.*

## ∷ SCIENTIFIC HISTORY

∷ In November 1997, the Brazilian self-styled bioartist Eduardo Kac created a performance artwork called 'Time Capsule'. This involved injecting a tiny capsule containing a radio frequency identification (RFID) tag (see also pages 121–123) under the skin of his right ankle. These ID capsules had previously been used to identify pets and other animals so they could be reunited with their owners when they got lost. Scanning the tag caused its transponder to transmit a unique 12-digit number that Kac then registered in a database of animals, with himself listed as both animal and owner. The whole thing was televised in a webcast.

In August 1998, Professor Kevin Warwick of the Department of Cybernetics at the University of Reading in England had a silicon chip transponder implanted under his skin using local anaesthetic. This was the beginning of 'Project Cyborg', where the professor's movement around the university campus was monitored and he could use the signal emitted by the chip to operate doors, lights, heating and computers without using his hands. The implant was removed after 10 days. In a second experiment in 2002, a new implant, this time an array of 100 electrodes, was inserted into the

| 1997_ |
| --- |
| Bioartist Eduardo Kac injects RFID tag into his ankle |

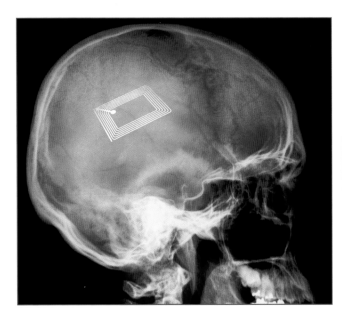

◀ RFID chips, which receive and transmit radio waves, could eventually be used to tag humans for security purposes.

**2003_**

Researchers develop chip to replace a rat's hippocampus

**2002_**

Warwick has 100 electrodes implanted into his arm

**1998_**

Kevin Warwick has a chip implanted under his skin

median nerves of Professor Warwick's left arm. During the three months in which the implant was left inside his arm, various tests were carried out. On one hand, the signals in the nerves were monitored when he carried out various activities. On the other, signals were sent to the electrodes to see what effect this would have. In the later stages of the project, signals from the implant were used to control a robotic hand, called a SNAVE hand, to apply a light touch to an object, and also to operate a motorised wheelchair.

## ⸬ SIGHTINGS IN SCI-FI

- The use of implants and biochips to enhance human abilities has been common in sci-fi since the 1960s.
- In Philip K Dick's 1966 short story 'We Can Remember It for You Wholesale' (filmed as *Total Recall*), artificial memories can be surgically implanted in people's brains.
- In 1972, the implanted wristwatch and telephone were created, in Larry Niven's story 'Cloak of

Anarchy' and Frank Herbert's novel *The Godmakers* respectively.

- Recently, the novel *Altered Carbon* (2003) by Richard Morgan introduced the 'cortical stack' – a memory stick that contains a 'backup' of your self, allowing personality and memories to be restored after death.

◀ Silicone chip transponders of the sort implanted into Professor Kevin Warwick. Implants may one day be used as an alternative to bank cards.

**2004_**

US Government develops VeriChip implant

## ⋗ REALITY

⋗ In 2003, Theodore Berger and a team at the University of Southern California in Los Angeles tested a microchip they had been developing for the previous 10 years that could be used to replace the hippocampus, the specific part of the brain dealing with the storage of new memories. They used the chip to stimulate sections of rat brain that had been kept alive artificially. The researchers are currently planning to implant the chips into live rats and monkeys who have had their hippocampi destroyed to see if they regain the ability to store new memories.

In October 2004, the US Food and Drug Administration (FDA) cleared the Verichip – a human-implantable microchip – for medical use. The VeriChip, which is about the size of a grain of rice, is inserted under the skin of the right tricep using a syringe. The chip itself is a passive RFID tag. The producers say the uses of the VeriChip include patient identification, access control and the management of human remains.

The following year, the European Group on Ethics in Science and New Technologies, an independent advisory group to the European Commission, expressed concern about the ethical aspects of implants into the human body. It warned of the privacy implications of a future in which data from implants, possibly regarding the subject's health, is transmitted to other parties. The group also said that implants should not be used to enhance physical and mental capabilities where this would create a two-class society, or to increase the gap between the industrialised countries and the rest of the world.

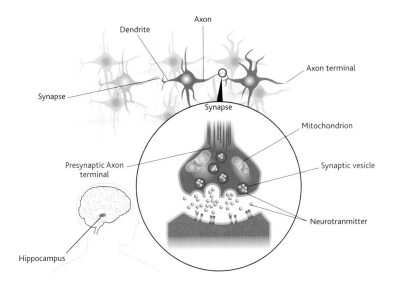

Before we can start adding to our memories in order to learn how to speak Mandarin or fly a helicopter, we need to know how the brain stores memories in the first place. Scientists know that the hippocampus has a role in long-term memory but there is still debate over exactly how it achieves this.

The hippocampus – so called because in cross-section it has the outline of a seahorse – sits in the medial temporal lobe of the brain. Humans, along with other mammals, have two hippocampi – one on each side of the brain. Much of the understanding of what the hippocampus does comes from people who have experienced damage to it, through oxygen starvation or diseases such as Alzheimer's or encephalitis. In particular, the study of a subject known only by the initials H M, enabled researchers to conclude that damage to the hippocampus did not affect IQ or the ability to learn procedures.

- Inside the hippocampus are millions of nerve cells called neurons, similar to those that pass nerve impulses around the rest of the brain.

- These cells are surrounded by membranes that selectively allow certain ions – salts of sodium,

potassium and chlorine, and various proteins – to cross into and out of the cell.

- These ions are electrically charged, as a result of having lost or gained electrons. Crossing the membrane causes the voltage difference between the inside and outside of the cell to change.

- Once the voltage has reached a specific threshold, the neuron fires, sending a signal to another neuron.

This electrochemical process is at the heart of how the brain works and stores memories.

The challenge for anyone making an artificial hippocampus is to replicate the function of these neurons. Theodore Berger and his team at the University of Southern California used a rat's brain, relatively simple compared to a human one, and applied electrical signals to every neuron in the brain tissue sample. They recorded the electrical response this caused in the sample and encoded this on their silicon chip. In this way, they were mimicking the action of the hippocampus without needing to know exactly what the brain was doing.

# PROBES
# AND SENSORS ⁖

*There comes a moment in most science fiction stories when the heroes scan a
seemingly abandoned spaceship for signs of life. The technology used in the sensors
or probes is conveniently glossed over but invariably they pick up energy sources
revealing silicon-based life forms. But it's not just science fiction: probes of a sort are
already here and one day the technology could be built into your mobile phone.*

## ⁖ SCIENTIFIC HISTORY

⁖ Sensing and probing in the sci-fi sense really means the detection of
various forms of electromagnetic radiation. With this in mind, the
history starts with Wilhelm Roentgen and the discovery of X-rays in
1895. Roentgen was carrying out experiments with cathode ray tubes
(used in televisions before plasma and LCD screens). In one
experiment he created an electrical discharge inside the tube. With
the lights off, he noticed a fluorescent effect on a screen treated with
barium platinocyanide; he put the effect down to a new form of
radiation that he called 'X-rays'. Soon afterward, he realised that X-
rays could be used to probe within the human body without surgery.

The modern era of detecting electromagnetic waves in the
infrared spectrum started during the Second World War. In 1917, T
W Case found that the compound thallous sulphide could be used
to detect infrared radiation and laid the foundations for thermal
imaging systems. Over the next four decades, scientists
experimented with various materials, and in 1958 W D Lawson and
his colleagues were the first to synthesise the compound mercury
cadmium telluride, which forms the basis of most thermal imaging
systems today.

> 1895_
>
> Wilhelm Roentgen discovers
> X-ray technology

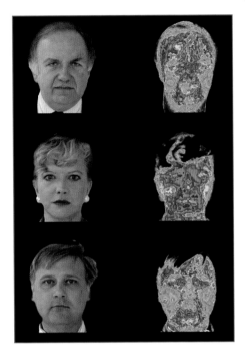

◀ With thermograms showing unique facial heat patterns, thermal skin imaging may be used for security access, or in conjunction with a police database, to identify known criminals.

1958_

Lawson group synthesises mercury cadmium telluride

1917_

T W Case uses thallous sulphide to detect infrared

## ⯈ REALITY

⯈ X-rays, radio waves and infrared (radiated heat) are all forms of photonic radiation, like visible light, that make up the electro-magnetic spectrum. Some of today's most interesting sensor technology comes from looking at the more unusual parts of this spectrum. Millimetre wave technology, for example, is increasingly used at ports and border crossings to identify smuggled objects, from guns to people.

## ⯈ SIGHTINGS IN SCI-FI

- A sensor that can detect the presence of living beings is used for military purposes in the 1958 short story 'Cease Fire', by Frank Herbert.

- In the 1960s, *Star Trek* popularised the idea of long- and short-range sensors for detecting life forms, energy levels, anomalies and alien ships and weapons.

- For deep-space data gathering outside the range of sensors, sci-fi often uses automated probes based on real-life NASA craft – for example at the beginning of *The Empire Strikes Back* (1980). This became a plot device in the first *Star Trek* movie (1979), in which one of NASA's Voyager probes returns to Earth centuries after it was launched.

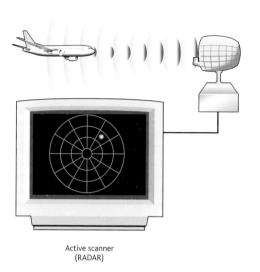

Active scanner
(RADAR)

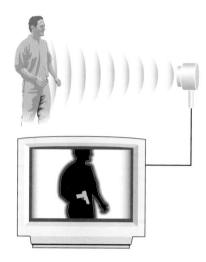

Passive scanner
(millimetre wave)

Detectors can be divided into two categories: passive and active.

- Active scanners emit energy and wait to see what reflections come back. It's a process copied from nature: bats use echolocation to make up for their poor eyesight, emitting high-frequency squeaks and building up a picture of the world around them by listening for the echoes. Dolphins do something similar with lower frequency sounds under water – this is also the basis for sonar used by submarines.

- Radar, invented in the 1930s, uses radio waves to scan for solid objects. The principle is the same as for other forms of active scanning: the radar tower sends out pulses and measures the echoes from aircraft, land-masses or whatever is being scanned.

- Passive scanners, by contrast, measure radiation naturally emitted by solid bodies. Rather than sending out pulses, they sit and wait for a signal to come to them.

- Passive millimetre wave scanners use the fact that virtually everything emits millimetre wave radiation, which is essentially extremely high-frequency radio waves. Different substances emit radiation in varying amounts: for example, human beings emit large amounts of millimetre wave radiation, while metals emit virtually none.

- Another key point is that millimetre waves pass through clothing without being absorbed.

- If you have tuned your scanner to detect millimetre wave radiation, and someone with a weapon concealed under their clothes stands in front of it, the metal of the gun will stand out against the body.

- The first commercial millimetre wave scanners were installed in Schiphol airport, in the Netherlands, in 2007.

# INVISIBILITY
# AND CLOAKING ⠶

*Being invisible could be fun – you could plant kisses on unsuspecting beautiful faces
or secretly listen in on gossipy conversations. But for military purposes, an invisibility
device would be invaluable. Stealth technologies – which make planes and tanks
almost invisible to radar – are improving all the time and a true cloaking shield may
not be so far off.*

## ⠶ SCIENTIFIC HISTORY

⠶ In 1862, the physicist James Clerk Maxwell first realised that visible
light was just one form of electromagnetic radiation. Early proposed
techniques for invisibility use this as their starting point – a material
that changes the wavelength of reflected light to somewhere
outside the visible spectrum would be effectively invisible to the
naked eye. However, science has yet to produce such a material.

| 1862_ |
| --- |
| Maxwell proposes that light is just one form of radiation |

Other theories focus on changing the refractive index of an
object – the measure of how much a beam of light is deflected
when it moves from one material into another – to render it
invisible. In 1967, Russian physicist Victor Veselago postulated that

## ⠶ SIGHTINGS IN SCI-FI

- The idea of invisibility was first popularised in
  fiction with H G Wells' *The Invisible Man* in 1897.

- The idea of 'cloaking' a spaceship so it is invisible
  to the eye and other sensory devices,
  such as radar, has only been around since the
  original 1960s *Star Trek*.

- The idea is mentioned, although not
  demonstrated, in 1980 in *The Empire Strikes Back*,
  while in the *Predator* movies (1987 and 1990),
  the aliens have a cloaking device that makes
  them virtually undetectable.

▲ SR-71 Blackbird, one of the first aircraft to be shaped to reduce radar cross section.

## 2006_

Researchers design an invisibility cloak

## 1970s_

First aircraft designed to escape radar detection

## 1967_

Veselago conceives materials with negative refractive index

## 1940s_

First stealth aircraft, the German Horten Ho IX

materials with a negative refractive index could exhibit strange optical properties but it is only in recent years that such materials – called 'metamaterials' – have been developed.

Military stealth technology focuses on deflecting radar waves. The German Horten Ho IX aircraft, built in the 1940s, is often considered the first stealth plane thanks to its flying wing design, which significantly reduced its radar profile. However, the first true stealth aircraft was Lockheed's Have Blue. Two prototypes were built in the late 1970s. The angled design was successful in fooling radar but less so in being aerodynamic – both prototypes crashed.

## ⠂ REALITY

⠂ Researchers from Duke University in North Carolina and Imperial College in London have demonstrated what they are calling the 'first practical realisation of an invisibility cloak', with which a copper cylinder was rendered invisible to microwave radiation. They are working to adapt the design for visible light.

Stealth aircraft have also continued to develop, from the SR-71 'Blackbird' (1964), to the F-117 'Nighthawk' (1983). Lockheed Martin's F-22 Raptor is the latest model: with low-profile wing and tail edges, and radar-absorbing surfaces, it has the radar signature of a bumblebee.

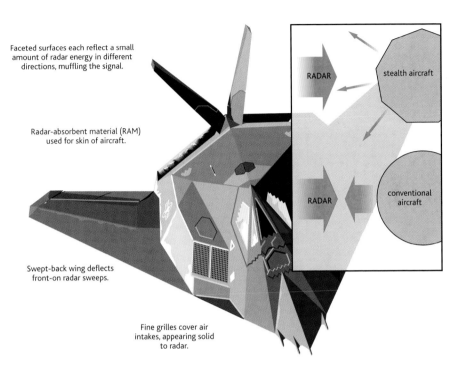

Faceted surfaces each reflect a small amount of radar energy in different directions, muffling the signal.

Radar-absorbent material (RAM) used for skin of aircraft.

Swept-back wing deflects front-on radar sweeps.

Fine grilles cover air intakes, appearing solid to radar.

RADAR — stealth aircraft

RADAR — conventional aircraft

- The theory behind the invisibility cloak designed at Duke University and Imperial College, London is based on metamaterials – materials whose electromagnetic properties depend on the structure of the object rather than the materials used. The cloak decreases scattering from the hidden object while at the same time reducing its shadow, so that the cloak and object combined begin to resemble free space. The flow of microwave radiation around the object is similar to the flow of water around a stick in a river.

- Stealth technology, in contrast, relies on absorbing or deflecting incoming radiation rather than bending electromagnetic waves around the plane. The surfaces of stealth planes typically fall into two categories: those with angled surfaces to scatter radar signals and those that are coated in radar-absorbing materials such as paint.

  - Jagged edges scatter reflected radio waves in different directions, thus reducing the radar echo.

  - Radar-absorbing paint contains small iron balls, which absorb radio waves and disperse them as heat rather than reflecting them back towards the radar detector.

# FORCE FIELDS AND SHIELDS⌇

*As weapons become increasingly potent, you need to be able to protect yourself with increasing robustness. The ultimate in sci-fi protection for humans and vehicles is a force field or shield. In recent years, researchers have carried out work on cold plasmas that has given tantalising glimpses of the technology to shield yourself against attack from future weapons such as laser beams and death rays.*

## ⋗SCIENTIFIC HISTORY

⋗ The concept of fields of force was first considered by Sir Isaac Newton when he conceived his universal law of gravitation, published in 1687 in his master work *Principia*.

Other forces of nature came under the scrutiny of English scientist Michael Faraday in the 19th century. Faraday's work with electricity and magnetism led him to map out the shape of a magnetic field, the first visual representation of a force field.

> **1687_**
>
> Sir Isaac Newton theorises fields of force

◀ A shield against ballistic missiles like this would transform modern warfare.

## ⋗SIGHTINGS IN SCI-FI

- Force fields and shields are very common and have changed very little since their introduction by E E 'Doc' Smith in some of his 'Amazing Stories' from the early 1930s.

- They were popularised in *Star Trek* in the 1960s. The fields, made up of a projected and largely invisible force, often function as a protective barrier or shield, small enough to cover a soldier or big enough to cover a spaceship or an entire planet. At other times, the shields can locally contain an explosion, fire or other threat (such as toxic gas).

- In the 1970s, the idea of a deflector shield – which shunted aside any energy fired at it – entered the sci-fi lexicon through *Star Wars*.

**1999_**

Plasma shielding technology is conceived

**1970s_**

Dr Manfred Held invents 'reactive armour'

**1940s_**

Shielding devices designed for aircraft instruments

**1830s_**

Michael Faraday introduces the idea of lines of force

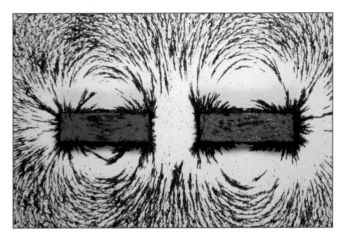

▲ A demonstration with iron filings to show the work of magnetic fields. Forcefield technology is based on these principles of lines of force.

The discovery that electromagnetic forces are all around us, and the sensitivity of modern electronics, led engineers to start thinking about magnetic and electrostatic shields that could protect equipment from electromagnetic interference. During the Second World War the Magnetic Shield Corporation built devices that could shield sensitive aircraft navigation instruments from outside interference. Following the invention of radar at around the same time, German and US scientists came up with stealth paint that absorbed the radio waves used by radar, so that planes could avoid detection (see pages 109–111). A more exciting announcement came in 1999 when Anatoliy Korteev of the Keldysh Research Centre in Russia announced details of research into plasma stealth technology. His team created a device that weighs less than 100 kilograms (220 pounds) but can generate a plasma field around an aircraft to confuse radar.

At the same time, the invention of increasingly devastating explosive ammunition prompted engineers to develop better forms of physical armour. In the 1970s, Dr Manfred Held came up with the concept of reactive armour, which uses two metal plates with a layer of explosive sandwiched between them. On impact, the explosive would detonate and the outer plate would be blown outwards, absorbing the kinetic energy of the incoming projectile. The inner plate would protect the vehicle from harm.

## ⠿ REALITY

⠿ At the Old Dominion University in Norfolk, Virginia, engineer Mounir Laroussi has been creating cold plasmas that have potential for a variety of uses, from cloaking technology for military aircraft, to a shield for orbiting satellites or, as a means of deflecting energy weapons based on electromagnetic radiation (including lasers and microwaves).

To produce his cold plasmas, Laroussi fills a Plexiglass cube with helium gas and ionises it (splits off electrons to create a charged 'soup' of material) by passing it between two electrodes with a high voltage difference between them. Unlike hot plasmas, which make up the outer layer of the Sun and can reach temperatures of several million degrees, Laroussi's plasmas are cold enough that you can put your hand in them with no ill effects. Because it is ionised, it responds to magnets, so a magnetic field could be used to hold it in place around a vehicle.

Any future shielding technology could combine plasma stealth technology, which absorbs various forms of electromagnetic radiation such as high-intensity microwaves or X-ray laser beams, with traditional defence technologies, such as reactive armour, that deals with incoming missiles, to create a tank that is invisible to radar and invulnerable to conventional attack. Technologies like these might allow us to one day say, with gusto, 'Raise the shields!'

## ⠿ TECH SPEC: FUTURE ARMOUR

Plasmas are considered the fourth state of matter, after liquids, solids and gases. In a plasma, the constituent atoms and molecules have been ionised, meaning they have had one or more electrons stripped off them to leave a 'soup' of positively charged ions and negatively charged electrons. Natural plasmas are common in the universe, making up as much as 99 per cent of all material. The Earth is surrounded by belts of plasma, including the ionosphere.

Plasmas are very good at absorbing and deflecting electromagnetic radiation. The plasma in the ionosphere, for example, enables you to hear radio stations even when you are not in the line of sight of the radio mast. With the right sort of plasma, electromagnetic radiation of all types, including X-rays and microwaves, could be absorbed and deflected – a very handy shield.

Reactive armour, on the other hand, works in one of two ways:

- Explosive armour, such as Russia's Kontakt-5, sandwiches an explosive material between two metal plates. On contact, the inner material explodes outwards, slowing down the projectile and sometimes destroying it.

- Non-explosive reactive armour uses an inert layer of rubber or similar material. This layer absorbs the projectile's kinetic energy, causing the armour to warp.

# HACKING
# AND MALWARE ⁘

*Powerful computers will always be a draw but future hackers and creators of malware – the collective name for a wealth of sophisticated hacking tools – are likely to target other devices such as mobile phones and MP3 players. With many items in our lives including computer processors, we should be very scared indeed.*

## ⮞ SCIENTIFIC HISTORY

⮞ The term 'hackers' emerged at MIT in the 1960s, where some of the first shared mainframe computers were being used. In the early days, hacking was not malicious but involved tweaking systems to make them work better.

The first computer virus to spread beyond an individual computer was called Elk Cloner, written by 15-year-old Rich Skrenta in 1982. The virus overwrote certain areas on floppy disks that would then cause a computer to be infected the 50th time it was

| 1960S_ |
| --- |
| The term 'hacker' emerges |

## ⮞ SIGHTINGS IN SCI-FI

- David Gerrold's 1972 novel *When H.A.R.L.I.E. Was One* predicted hacking through telephone lines: an artificial intelligence uses a virus to invade other computers, reprogramme them and return with users' private information.

- In John Brunner's 1975 novel *The Shockwave Rider*, an outlaw creates self-contained computer software that collects secret government

information; Brunner also coined the term 'worm', which stands for 'Write Once, Read Many times.'

- The movies *War Games* (1983) and *Sneakers* (1992) were early films to popularise computer hacking. In the the *Matrix* films in the 1990s and 2000s, Agent Smith develops a virus to transform all entities he touches into his likeness.

started up from the disk. Since then, e-mail viruses have raised their ugly heads, as have self-replicating Internet worms, spyware (software that is installed on users' systems without their knowledge to monitor what the computers are doing) and adware (spyware that makes pop-up ads appear while the user is browsing the Internet). By 2002, peer-to-peer applications such as Kazaa and Instant Messenger were being used to propagate computer viruses.

## ⊱ REALITY

⊱ Antivirus company McAfee announced in 2006 that the number of different types of threats in its database, including viruses, spyware and malware, had risen to 200,000. New threats are appearing faster than ever. The company says it took 18 years to reach 100,000 threats but just two years to record the next 100,000.

While viruses used to be created by some hackers for fun or as a challenge, increasingly they are being used to make money. Trojans threaten to delete files from a user's computer unless a ransom is paid. The use of Trojans and worms to turn computers into zombies – performing malicious tasks on behalf of others – is also increasing. By far the most common use of zombies is as distributors of e-mail spam; meanwhile fake websites dedicated to celebrities are becoming the most common source of malware.

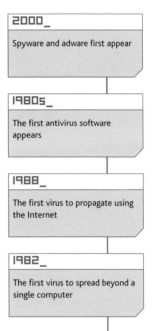

**2000_**
Spyware and adware first appear

**1980s_**
The first antivirus software appears

**1988_**
The first virus to propagate using the Internet

**1982_**
The first virus to spread beyond a single computer

## ⊱ TECH SPEC: MALWARE

Each type of threat – virus, Trojan, worm – works in a subtly different way.

- Boot sector viruses, named after the area on a floppy disk or hard drive which contained the code to boot up the computer, were the first to appear. A boot sector virus would overwrite this code with an infected version, which would then cause the computer to malfunction.

- Macro viruses, of which the famous 1999 Melissa virus was one, use the advanced features of applications such as Microsoft Word and Excel. The macro feature of these applications allows users to run mini-programs from within the application environment, for example to do a repetitive task. By tinkering with the template document from these

applications, the macro virus causes the macro to run as soon as the document is opened, wreaking havoc on your computer.

- Trojans are computer programs that appear to do one thing – such as play a game or run a useful application – while doing another – infecting your computer to corrupt data, make it run slowly, disable it completely or forward the Trojan to other unsuspecting computer users.

- Unlike viruses and Trojans, worms do not need human intervention to start working. Instead, they tend to rely on bugs and loopholes in operating systems, particularly Microsoft Windows, and network software, such as Microsoft Internet Explorer.

# SPY CAMS
# AND SURVEILLANCE ⋖

*Do you ever feel as if you are being watched? You should. CCTV (closed-circuit television) is on the rise worldwide. In an ideal world, CCTV cameras would reduce crime but some argue that they just push the problem elsewhere. Civil libertarians also worry about how far these devices intrude into people's privacy.*

## ⋗ SCIENTIFIC HISTORY

⋗ The history of CCTV is almost as old as the history of television itself. It was one of television's pioneers who demonstrated closed-circuit television for the first time: at the Hairdressing Fair of Fashion in 1930, John Logie Baird used CCTV to show advertisements for a hair product. CCTV for industrial purposes arrived in the 1940s when Diamond Electronics invented the Utiliscope, which monitored water levels in boilers.

The first system that used CCTV to monitor traffic lights was set up in the northern English city of Durham in 1956, but the real boom came in the 1960s, when the video cassette recorder first became available. Before this, saving images for later viewing was only possible by developing film – a slow and costly process. Magnetic video storage also gave rise to the use of CCTV for surveillance. In 1960, London's Metropolitan Police set up two pan, tilt and zoom cameras in Trafalgar Square to monitor crowds watching a state visit to Parliament. Police forces in the United States began using CCTV for surveillance a few years later.

> 1930_
>
> Baird uses CCTV to broadcast advertisements

## ⋗ REALITY

⋗ CCTV has taken off in the biggest way in the UK – a recent survey of Europe estimated that the number of systems operating in the UK

◄ Some CCTV systems are paired with smart software to detect or predict suspicious behaviour

**1960S_**

Video recording equipment becomes available

**1956_**

First CCTV system to monitor traffic lights

**1950S_**

Penn State University gives lectures by CCTV

**1947_**

Ohio Power Company uses CCTV to monitor water levels

was a staggering four million, around 10 per cent of the total systems in operation worldwide.

CCTV cameras are becoming active rather than passive devices. In the Wiltshire, CCTV cameras fitted with speakers were installed at an industrial park that was beset with crime problems. Operators monitoring the cameras from 64 kilometres (40 miles) away could then use the speakers to bark orders at anyone seen committing a crime.

The move from videotape to digital media has had its impact on the world of CCTV, where DVD recorders and hard-disk drive recorders are becoming common, and the price of data storage

## ⸱ SIGHTINGS IN SCI-FI

- The idea of Big Brother watching you through your Telescreen made its debut in George Orwell's dystopic 1948 novel *1984* but there were earlier technologies for surveillance, such as Spy Rays in 1930s pulp sci-fi.

- In 1941, Robert Heinlein saw that a traffic-control camera might be useful; in the 1960s, Jack Vance predicted the robotic 'stick-tight', a device that follows a subject and records video; and Robert Silverberg used the metaphor of a recording eye

in the late 1960s as something deployed from space that transmits data back.

- In the world of *Star Trek*, mechanical probes are sent out to scan and videotape the outside world, and to return with their findings.

- Spy cams became really interesting in the 1985 James Bond movie *A View to a Kill*, in which Bond has a spy cam in his ring.

continues to fall. The Internet has also had a major impact on the development of CCTV in recent years. Network CCTV allows cameras to be linked to a computer and the footage dumped to a hard drive rather than video tape.

CCTV is also combined with other technologies to make it more powerful. Smart CCTV uses facial recognition technology so that criminals caught on camera can be identified by comparison with a police database. Casinos around the world have also used smart CCTV to catch card counters and other cheats.

Surveillance cameras are also showing up in the home, thanks to the rise of the cheap webcam. Now you can keep an eye on your house and its contents, or maybe even the nanny while she looks after your kids, when you're at work or travelling – anywhere you can get an Internet connection. Some systems even let you watch the footage from the webcam on your mobile phone.

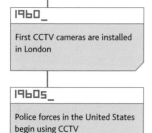

**1960_**

First CCTV cameras are installed in London

**1960s_**

Police forces in the United States begin using CCTV

---

## >TECH SPEC: CCTV

- Since all of the elements of a CCTV system are connected, one of the key issues is range. CCTV systems typically use coaxial cable – cable containing a central conducting wire surrounded by an insulating material and another conductor made of tube or braid – to transmit their signal. The cable used in most CCTV systems can carry signals for up to a few hundred metres. Fibre-optic and twisted-pair cables, which incorporate several pairs of wires that are twisted together to reduce signal decay, are increasingly being used to extend the range of CCTV systems to distances of several kilometres. And as more CCTV systems begin to incorporate Wi-Fi technology (see pages 90–94), range becomes even less of an issue.

- Many CCTV systems use time-lapse recording to capture just one or two frames of video every second. This ensures that most criminal acts can be observed but the need for vast amounts of storage is reduced. Some time-lapse VCRs can record more than a thousand hours of surveillance onto a standard video tape using this method. These days, many CCTV cameras are linked to motion-detection devices as well. This means that images are only recorded when someone or something is moving within the field of view of the camera.

- Even with time-lapse recording and motion detection, the amount of data is still considerable. Network CCTV often uses video compression techniques such as MPEG-4 to reduce the amount of storage required even further. At a rough estimate, a system with four cameras, recording with MPEG-4 compression at 30 frames per second and a resolution of 320 by 240, only active when there is motion in front of the cameras, for 16 hours a day, five days a week, would use up about 20 to 25 GB of disk space every week – that's enough to fill about 25 CD-ROMs.

# 04:08_

# TRACKING DEVICES ⊰

*It's the faint smell of aftershave on her neck or the smallest trace of lipstick on his collar that sets you thinking that your spouse is having an affair. Hiring a private detective is too expensive but what about using some sort of tracking device to find out whether your loved one really is in the office until midnight? With tracking devices becoming smaller and smaller, you might be able to slip something into his or her briefcase without raising suspicions and watch the infidelity unfold on an Internet mapping site.*

## ⊱SCIENTIFIC HISTORY

⊱ Mario Cardullo came up with the idea of radio frequency identification (RFID) tags in 1969, while discussing car tracking systems with an IBM engineer. He envisioned a tag that incorporated a transmitter, a receiver, internal memory and power source. The idea was patented in 1973.

While RFID tags are good for tracking things over short distances, they do not provide a solution to tracking on a global scale. For this,

## ⊱SIGHTINGS IN SCI-FI

- The miniaturised tracking device, or homing beacon, was popularised in *Batman* and *Spider-Man* comics, as well as spy novels, throughout the 1960s and 1970s.

- James Bond had two different tracking devices in *Goldfinger* (1964): one he attaches to Goldfinger's car and the other is hidden in the heel of his shoe.

- In *Star Wars* (1977), Darth Vader orders a tracking beacon attached to the *Millennium Falcon* so he can follow the spaceship back to the Rebels' base of operations.

- In the *RoboCop* TV series (1994), police pistols can fire tracking pellets instead of bullets into escaping criminals, to follow their location remotely.

we had to wait until 1993, when the Global Positioning System (GPS) was launched. Officially named NAVSTAR GPS, this global navigating system had been under development as a military project by the US Department of Defense. With the launch of GPS, any device equipped with the necessary decoding technology could communicate with a constellation of microwave-transmitting satellites to work out exactly where it was on the Earth's surface. NAVSTAR GPS was declared fully operational in 1995, and in 1996, US President Bill Clinton issued a policy directive opening GPS to civilian as well as military use.

## ⫶ REALITY

⫶ RFID tags have found numerous uses since they were invented and are particularly popular in the retail setting, where goods can be fitted with cheap tags to help store managers control their inventory and discourage shoplifting.

The technology is also used in travel and transportation: McCarran International Airport in Las Vegas uses RFID tags to track the movement of baggage through the airport. Traditionally, airports have used barcode tags attached to bags, which are scanned as they pass through the baggage-handling system. However, the barcode, unlike RFID tags, needs to be in the line of sight of the scanner to work. RFID chips are also being used in the new generation of e-passports.

Use of GPS has also grown hugely since its launch. Virtually every new car that rolls off the production line includes satellite navigation and many old cars are being upgraded with handheld devices. Just as Internet map sites took over from printed roadmaps, more powerful satnav devices now threaten to take over map websites. A firm called Strategy Analytics estimates that 18 million GPS devices were sold worldwide in 2005 and that this number will rise to 88 million a year by 2010. The launch of a European rival to GPS called Galileo will help to boost this number, and other countries are also developing satellite navigation networks: China is proposing to expand its Beidou regional system into a global one, while Russia is developing GLONASS.

On a more personal level, two billion people around the world already carry a tracking device around without realising it – their mobile phones. Because of the cellular radio system used by mobile phones, your location can be pinpointed to within a few hundred feet when you carry one.

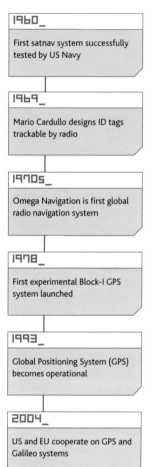

**1960_**

First satnav system successfully tested by US Navy

**1969_**

Mario Cardullo designs ID tags trackable by radio

**1970s_**

Omega Navigation is first global radio navigation system

**1978_**

First experimental Block-I GPS system launched

**1993_**

Global Positioning System (GPS) becomes operational

**2004_**

US and EU cooperate on GPS and Galileo systems

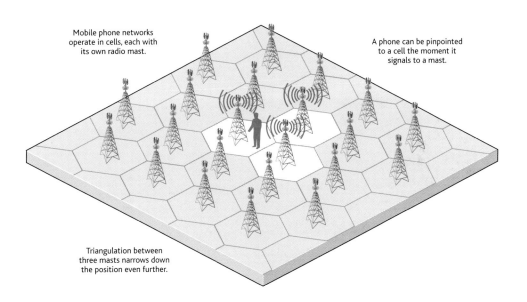

Mobile phone networks operate in cells, each with its own radio mast.

A phone can be pinpointed to a cell the moment it signals to a mast.

Triangulation between three masts narrows down the position even further.

Location-based services on your mobile phone work by one of two methods.

The first method uses the cellular nature of mobile phone networks:

- The network is made up of individual cells, each centred on a radio mast. The size of a cell depends on the topography of the area but can be anything up to a few square kilometres.

- When your phone is on, the cell you are currently using can be tracked, pinpointing your location.

The second, more accurate method involves triangulating between a number of masts:

- Your mobile phone can usually be 'seen' by a number of different masts.

- By measuring the signal strengths and the time delay in signals received from the phone at various masts, the phone's location can be pinpointed to within a few hundred feet.

# BIOLOGICAL AND
# CHEMICAL WARFARE ◁

*Conventional weapons of mass destruction can be complicated and expensive.
Instead, what better way to kill off your enemies than to introduce a small amount
of biological agent into their water supply or release a nerve gas into their mass
transport network?*

## ⯈ SCIENTIFIC HISTORY

⯈ In 1877, German bacteriologist Robert Koch isolated the bacterium
*Bacillus anthracis* and proved that it caused the disease anthrax in
cattle – the first time a bacterium had been conclusively shown to
cause a specific disease. The chemical tabun, discovered by accident
by Dr Gerhard Schräder when he was studying chemicals known as
organophosphates in Germany in 1936, was the first of the so-called
G-series of nerve agents. Others, including sarin and cyclosarin,
followed during and after the Second World War.

## ⯈ SIGHTINGS IN SCI-FI

- In H G Wells' classic 1898 novel *War of the Worlds*,
  it is the invisible microorganisms in the air –
  which Wells called 'the humblest things that God,
  in his wisdom, has put upon this earth' – that
  finally stop the Martians. Michael Crichton's 1969
  thriller *The Andromeda Strain* reversed this idea:
  what if the disease came from space and attacked
  humans?

- Frank Herbert's 1982 novel *The White Plague*
  follows a man who, having lost his wife and
  children, creates a disease that kills only women.

- Movies that have looked at the repercussions of
  biological weapons include *The Stand* (1994),
  *Twelve Monkeys* (1995), *Outbreak* (1995) and *28
  Days Later (2002)*.

◀ Police officer wearing a chemical protection suit. After 9/11, anthrax scares focused people's attention on the prospect of bioterrorism.

## ⋗ REALITY

⋗ A US National Defense University study on bioterrorism and biocrimes found that in the majority of incidents involving biological and chemical agents, use was threatened rather than actually carried out: fewer than 20 per cent involved criminal groups obtaining nerve agents and going on to use them. One of the most high-profile of these incidents was the Japanese cult Aum Shinrikyo's sarin gas attack on the Tokyo subway system in 1995, which killed 12 and hospitalised 5,000.

By 2005, 171 countries had signed the 1972 Biological and Toxin Weapons Convention, which aims to prohibit the development, production and stockpiling of chemical and biological weapons. However, there is no apparatus in place for monitoring compliance with the Convention and some of the signatory countries are suspected of having used such weapons.

## ⋗ TECH SPEC: NERVE GAS

The contraction and relaxation of muscles in the body is controlled by chemicals known as neurotransmitters:

- When the nervous system wants a muscle to contract, a neurotransmitter called 'acetylcholine' is released.

- When the nervous system wants a muscle to relax, an enzyme called 'acetylcholine esterase' breaks the neurotransmitter down.

- When humans are exposed to nerve agents such as sarin and tabun, through contact with the skin or eyes or by ingesting them, the production of the enzyme is stopped. This means the signal to the muscles to contract continues uninterrupted.

- Symptoms can appear anywhere between a few seconds and several hours after exposure and can be anything from eye pain and weakness to convulsions and respiratory failure, leading to death.

# FUTURE WEAPONS ⁘_

*Science fiction has given us some pretty cool weapons but the reality is often stranger than fiction: governments are spending billions of dollars on everything from antimatter weapons to swarms of nanoscopic robot soldiers. Combined with future exoskeleton technology and force fields, the future fighter will be an awesome force to be reckoned with.*

## ⁘ SCIENTIFIC HISTORY

Primates used sticks and stones to fight off others when in search of food, and the race to find better weapons has not stopped since. While gunpowder emerged from China in the 11th century, and the gun a couple of centuries later, the development of deadly future weapons really began in the 20th century.

Antimatter was first postulated by the scientist Paul Dirac in 1928 and was seen for the first time in 1932, when Carl A Anderson found evidence for the positron, the antimatter equivalent of the electron (see pages 20–21). In 1940, the first blueprint for an atomic bomb was created, leading to the Manhattan Project.

> **1940_**
>
> First blueprint for an atomic bomb drawn up

## ⁘ SIGHTINGS IN SCI-FI

- Sci-fi has long been fascinated by energy weapons. The Martians in H G Wells' 1898 novel *The War of the Worlds* used heat rays to destroy the pinnacle of 19th-century technology.

- In the 1930s Buck Rogers used a ray gun, and in *Flash Gordon*, the evil Emperor Ming the Merciless used death rays.

- With the invention of the laser in the 1960s, death rays found a scientific basis. Photon torpedos and phasers appeared in *Star Trek*, while *Star Wars* (1977) united ancient and futuristic technology in the lightsabre and gave us the ultimate weapon: the *Death Star*, with an energy weapon that could destroy a planet.

In the early 1950s, the United States unveiled the Nike Ajax, the world's first ground-based supersonic guided missile. In 1957, the first step in the development of space-based weapons took place with the launch by the Russians of the first artificial satellite, *Sputnik*. Later that decade, the particle physicist Richard Feynmann first discussed the concept of nanotechnology. The laser, which would go on to generate more mentions in science fiction books and movies than perhaps any other device, appeared in 1960 and the world's first rail gun, which used magnetic acceleration as its operating principle, was built by John P Barber and Richard A Marshall in the early 1970s.

## ⋗ REALITY

⋗ Future weapons development is a big and expensive business, with many countries running programmes, including the United States' Land Warrior and the UK's Future Infantry Soldier Technology (FIST). The money required for this is staggering. In the United States' defence budget for 2007, some US$63 billion was put aside just for weapons development, out of a total budget of US$440 billion.

So what is the money being spent on? The answers are mostly kept secret. But in 2004, it was reported that Kenneth Edwards, director of the 'revolutionary munitions' team at Eglin Air Force Base in Florida, spoke about antimatter technologies at a speech for the NASA Institute for Advanced Concepts, the agency's arm for funding futuristic aeronautic and space technologies.

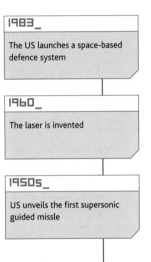

**1983_**
The US launches a space-based defence system

**1960_**
The laser is invented

**1950s_**
US unveils the first supersonic guided missile

## ⋗TECH SPEC: ANTIMATTER WEAPONS

- Antimatter weapons use one basic principle for their deadliness – antimatter annihilates on contact with ordinary matter to release energy.

- Ordinary matter is made up of building blocks, such as the electron and proton. For every particle there is a corresponding antiparticle. The electron's counterpart is called the positron, in recognition that it has a positive charge compared to the electron's negative one. The proton's antimatter partner is the antiproton.

- When a particle bumps into its antiparticle, they both annihilate in a shower of photons of electromagnetic radiation. It is this radiation that future weapons designers want to tap.

- However, the big problem with antimatter is how to contain it, since any contact with corresponding matter particles will cause it to annihilate – not particularly useful if you are holding the weapon in your hand. Magnetic fields may be the answer.

# LIFE, HEALTH AND SEX⋲

The future is where we will spend the rest of our lives – but how exactly will we spend them? Where will we live, work, sleep and play? What will we eat and drink? Will virtual sex partners undo matrimony as we know it? What ethical quandaries will we face? Will we embrace cloning and genetic engineering? And how about ending that whole famine, poverty and disease thing? We could end up with the technological wonderland of our wildest dreams but it won't mean much if our quality of life suffers in the process. We have a responsibility to look after this world, not only for ourselves but also for those who will come after us and this may not be easily accomplished. Futurists are brimming with dystopic visions of tomorrow, warning that our ethics may not be as advanced as our science; by contrast, forecasts of pure utopia are in short supply.

Nevertheless, as a species we are up to the challenge: thankfully, the drive to improve our condition remains an essential part of our humanity and if we can make each successive day even a little bit better than the one that came before, we might just achieve the promise of the future.

◀ Jane Fonda as Barbarella in the 1968 movie, one of many erotic characters from classic sci-fi.

# TELEMEDICINE ⋰

*If media scare stories are anything to go by, we are all obsessed with our health. Despite this obsession, many people are afraid of going to see the doctor for fear of what they might discover. Soon we will worry no more: our vital signs will be monitored remotely and, if anything abnormal happens, your friendly, holographic, computer-generated doctor will pop up to alleviate your concerns, or even start surgery right there in your home.*

## ⋰ SCIENTIFIC HISTORY

⋰ Telemedicine, the real-time transmission of medical data, started with the invention of the telephone in 1865 and developed with the invention of radio later that century. In 1903, Dutch physiologist Willem Einthoven created a highly sensitive galvanometer, which he used to record the electrical activity of the heart. In 1905, Einthoven began transmitting signals from this apparatus across telephone lines from the hospital to his laboratory a mile away, allowing him to monitor patients remotely.

## ⋰ SIGHTINGS IN SCI-FI

- In the original *Star Trek*, Dr 'Bones' McCoy was provided with both hospital beds that monitored key body functions without messy wires or tubes, and the 'tricorder', a machine that could instantly diagnose, treat and heal damaged tissues using energy instead of surgery.

- Larry Niven's *Ringworld* (1970) included the 'autodoc', an automated physician.
- In *Star Trek: Voyager* (1995), Robert Picardo played an emergency medical hologram (EMH), programmed with the sum of human medical knowledge as well as futuristic physician's techniques.

NASA began work on telemedicine in the 1960s with the *Mercury* Earth-orbit programme. Satellite links allowed ground crews to monitor the medical status of astronauts in orbit. The big boost for telemedicine came in the 1970s and 1980s with the development of videoconferencing, allowing high-quality video to be beamed across great distances. In September 2001, the first major telesurgery – the removal of a gall bladder – took place, with a surgeon in New York controlling a robot arm in Strasbourg, France.

Holography was conceived by Hungarian physicist Dennis Gabor in 1947. However, early holograms were distorted and contained an extra twin image because of the limitations of the light source used. The invention of the laser in 1958 at Bell Labs, USA changed all that but science has not yet been able to create a three-dimensional image that you can look at from any angle.

## ⫶ REALITY

⫶ Telemedicine and telehealth are now big business – some estimate that the industry is worth US$30 billion a year. A major factor has been the recent explosion in the number of home computers and the emergence of broadband connections, which have allowed sophisticated telemedicine applications to flourish.

Although the computer power and telecommunications links are in place to enable many aspects of telemedicine, access to a three-dimensional holographic doctor is still some way off. Hologram technology can currently only produce images from one angle, and the artificial intelligence necessary to diagnose any disease – let alone perform surgery – has yet to be developed.

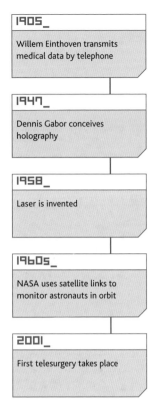

**1905_**
Willem Einthoven transmits medical data by telephone

**1947_**
Dennis Gabor conceives holography

**1958_**
Laser is invented

**1960s_**
NASA uses satellite links to monitor astronauts in orbit

**2001_**
First telesurgery takes place

## ⫶ TECH SPEC: 3D HOLOGRAMS

Three-dimensional visualisation systems do exist, although typically they use bulky equipment – spinning screens, light sources or hidden mirrors – to achieve the effect. One of the more promising technologies is the cathode ray sphere, developed by Barry Blundell and a team at the University of Canterbury in New Zealand in the 1990s:

• The cathode ray sphere is a sphere from which all the air has been evacuated.

• A phosphor-coated screen rotates within the sphere.

• Voxels – the three-dimensional equivalent of pixels – are drawn on the screen using two electron beams.

• The phosphor screen spins fast enough to give the illusion of a 3D image.

• The view seen from outside changes as the eye position moves, giving important clues about visual depth and making the image appear solid.

# BIONIC BODY PARTS ‹

*Ever since Steve Austin became the 'Six Million Dollar Man', people everywhere have dreamed of being bionically enhanced to be able to see further, run faster and jump higher. Scientists are gradually learning how to connect electronically controlled prostheses to the human central nervous system. The next-generation prosthetic will even be able to re-create the sense of touch, feeding back information to the wearer. One day, prosthetic limbs may even exceed the human parts they replace and those dreams of bionic enhancement will be fulfilled.*

## ›SCIENTIFIC HISTORY

› Artificial body parts have been around for millennia. Herodotus, in the fifth century BCE, described a man with a wooden leg and an Egyptian mummy with a wooden toe was discovered in 2007. The large number of amputees returning from the Second World War and the polio epidemic of the 1950s, spurred the development of modern prosthetics. In 1963 a robotic arm for the handicapped was developed at Rancho Los Amigos Hospital, Downey, California.

As well as limbs, prosthetic internal organs have been developed. The world's first pacemaker was invented at the National Research Council of Canada in 1949 by Jack Hopps. The device operated on grid electricity and was very uncomfortable for patients. Developments in the 1950s led to more comfortable battery-powered pacemakers that could be implanted under the skin.

1940s_

Modern prosthetics developed
Second World War

## ›REALITY

› Lungs are now getting the bionic treatment too. In 2001, Dr Brack Hattler of the University of Pittsburgh unveiled an artificial lung —

◀ Prosthetic limbs can now be used by professional athletes.

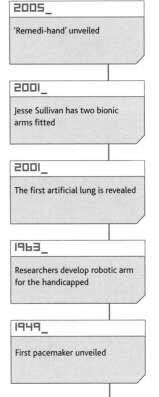

**2005_**

'Remedi-hand' unveiled

**2001_**

Jesse Sullivan has two bionic arms fitted

**2001_**

The first artificial lung is revealed

**1963_**

Researchers develop robotic arm for the handicapped

**1949_**

First pacemaker unveiled

the Hattler Respiratory Catheter – that can be implanted in the patient, oxygenating blood that passes through it. However, the device can only be worn for two weeks, so is suited to those with temporary rather than permanent lung damage.

Jesse Sullivan, a 54-year-old power worker, became the first person to get truly 'bionic' arms back in 2001. Dr Todd Kuiken of the Rehabilitation Institute of Chicago developed the arms, which were grafted to nerves and muscle so that they could be controlled by thought.

In late 2005, researchers at the University of Southampton revealed a next-generation bionic hand. It included motors and gears which allowed each finger to move independently. The device also featured the world's first robotic opposable thumb, allowing the 'Remedi-hand' to grip objects.

## ▷ SIGHTINGS IN SCI-FI

- In Robert Henlein's 1959 novel *Starship Troopers*, human infantry regularly suffer the loss of limbs in their battles with aliens and mechanical replacements are a fact of life.
- Steve Austin in the 1970s TV series *The Six Million Dollar Man* is often referred to as 'the bionic man'.

- In recent works such as Neal Stephenson's *The Diamond Age* (1995) or the influential video game series *Deus Ex* (2000), bionics takes the form of nano-augmentation – infusions of microscopic machines into the blood that provide healing or superhuman powers.

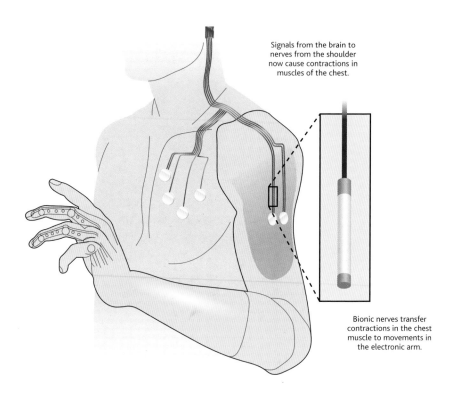

Signals from the brain to nerves from the shoulder now cause contractions in muscles of the chest.

Bionic nerves transfer contractions in the chest muscle to movements in the electronic arm.

Jesse Sullivan was the first man to have bionic arms fitted, following an accident involving high-voltage power lines that meant he had to have both arms amputated.

- Four nerves that used to go into his arms were dissected from his shoulder and grafted to muscles in his chest.

- The nerves grew into the chest muscles, so that when Sullivan thinks 'close hand', a portion of his chest muscle contracts.

- Surface electrodes then sense this chest activity to drive electrical signals in the bionic arm.

- This method of operation allows for simultaneous movement of the hand, wrist and elbow, unlike previous models.

After initial training, Sullivan was able to put on socks, shave, eat dinner and carry groceries, among other things that were previously impossible without assistance.

# SICK BAY ⋞

*One of the big problems with diagnosing the sick is that the tests to find out what is wrong are generally quite specific. Usually, a doctor makes a preliminary diagnosis before ordering the appropriate scan to confirm it. Think how much quicker diagnosis would be if a quick scan with a single device could reveal all.*

## ⋗ SCIENTIFIC HISTORY

⋗ In 1628, the British physician William Harvey outlined how blood flowed around the body. From that date on, doctors have analysed the blood because it contains proteins and cells from all around the human body. Automated blood analysis took a step forward in 1986 when Dr Imant Lauks invented the first silicon chip-based analyser.

X-rays were discovered at the end of the 19th century by Wilhelm Roentgen. He was experimenting with cathode ray tubes – similar to the tubes in pre-flatscreen televisions – when he noticed that a plate coated with the chemical barium platinocyanide glowed briefly when the tube was turned on. Even when the tube was covered with black card, he saw the glow. He called the mysterious phenomenon X-rays.

Nuclear magnetic resonance (NMR) was discovered in the 1940s. It was first used in the medical field in the 1970s, when Raymond Damadian showed that different types of tissue in the body reacted differently to strong magnetic fields. This opened up the possibility of using NMR for medical scanning. Paul Lauterbur demonstrated magnetic resonance imaging (MRI) for the first time on test tube samples in 1973.

At around the same time, the first computed axial tomography (CAT or CT) scanners started to appear. These create images of the body using an X-ray source and detector that rotate around the

> **1895_**
>
> Wilhelm Roentgen discovers X-rays

subject. Each rotation creates an image of a slice of the body; these are collated to create a three-dimensional image.

## ⋗ REALITY

⋗ In 2005, researchers at Kyushu University and the Japanese robotics company Tmsuk, developed a healthcare robot for use at theme parks and other public facilities that are difficult to reach by ambulance. Anyone sitting inside the robot has their pulse, blood pressure, heartbeat and blood oxygen level monitored. The robot sends the information to a hospital or first-aid centre, where a doctor can treat the problem by giving instructions to the patient or to bystanders.

Tmsuk has also developed three robots for Aizu Central Hospital that can respond to spoken instructions, carry luggage and guide patients to the relevant part of the hospital. The robots move around by detecting coloured stripes printed on the hospital floor, and avoid collisions by scanning around themselves 40 times a second with a low-intensity laser.

A more advanced robot took control of the world's first robotic operation in May 2006 at Milan's San Raffaele University. The robot, which has since carried out at least 40 operations guided by human surgeons, successfully operated on a 34-year-old patient suffering from atrial fibrillation after initial preparations were made by a human doctor.

A portable blood diagnosis kit that soldiers can carry with them on the battlefield is the goal of researchers at MIT's Institute for Soldier Nanotechnologies. In 2006, they announced a technique to create miniature pumps that could push blood through tiny channels engraved on a chip using battery power alone. The idea is

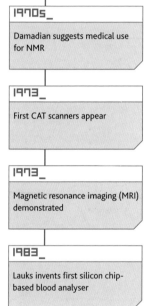

**1970s_**

Damadian suggests medical use for NMR

**1973_**

First CAT scanners appear

**1973_**

Magnetic resonance imaging (MRI) demonstrated

**1983_**

Lauks invents first silicon chip-based blood analyser

## ⋗ SIGHTINGS IN SCI-FI

- Sci-fi medical utopia appears in *Star Trek*, in which doctors can identify and undo any biological damage in matters of days, if not minutes.

- In 1959, Alan E Nourse's *Star Surgeon* showed what might be in store for doctors of the future, human and alien.

- The *Sector General* novels of James White, published from 1963, describe events on board a vast space station hospital.

- More recently, *Stardoc* (2000) is the first in a series of novels by S L Viehl about a surgeon leaving Earth to work at a distant colony clinic.

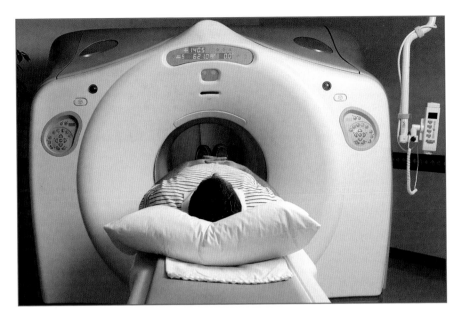

that a soldier would be able to analyse a minute drop of blood on the chip and have the results almost instantaneously, rather than having to send the sample off to a lab for analysis. Radiation sickness, chemical attack and diseases due to infected wounds or biological weapons could all be diagnosed on the spot, and give medics on the scene an instant reading of blood sugar levels and other key measurements of bodily health.

▲ An MRI scanner builds up images of the inside of the human body.

## ⟩TECH SPEC: MRI SCANNERS

MRI scanners use nuclear magnetic resonance to image the body:

- Protons – the positively charged constituents of the atomic nucleus – have an inherent property known as 'spin'.

- When protons are subjected to strong magnetic fields, perhaps 50,000 times the strength of the Earth's, the protons start to spin in a direction parallel or antiparallel to the field.

- If the proton encounters radio waves of the right frequency, its spin flips between these directions.

- When the proton flips back again naturally, a photon of electromagnetic radiation is released.

- This is detected by the scanner and used to build up an image with detail as small as a millimetre across.

- The absorption of the radio waves tells doctors much about the type of tissue being scanned – for example, whether it is healthy or diseased.

MRI scans are particularly good for scanning soft tissue, like the brain, spine, muscles and tendons.

# CLONING ⠿

*Humans are just too fragile – they get sick, have accidents and grow old. Cloning could well be the answer. Scientists would take a cell from your ear, add some nutrients and implant the growing ball of cells into a willing surrogate mother. Nine months later your clone would be ready and you could pick and choose healthy blood, tissue and body parts to replace the ones you've worn out.*

## ⠿ SCIENTIFIC HISTORY

⠿ Cloning, or the exact replication of a gene, cell or organism, has a long history. In fact, nature has been cloning since the very beginning. DNA, the building block of cellular life-forms, is a self-replicating molecule that creates cloned copies of itself for the purposes of cell division – one of the first steps on the road to life. Plants have long been good at cloning themselves: when you take a leaf cutting from a neighbour's garden, the plant that eventually grows in your own garden will be a clone of – genetically identical to – the original plant.

1938_

Spemann's *Embryonic Development and Induction*

The artificial cloning of animals began in Germany. In 1938 the embryologist Hans Spemann, who had won the Nobel Prize in 1935 for his work on embryonic development, published *Embryonic Development and Induction* in which he presented the results of his experiments into the transfer of the nucleus (where DNA is stored) from one living cell into another. He proposed that the next logical area of research would be into the cloning of living organisms. This prediction came true in the 1950s, when Robert Briggs and Thomas J King developed a technique to transplant nuclei from an embryonic northern leopard frog into the fertilised egg of another frog of the same species. In 1952, the pair demonstrated that eggs with transplanted nuclei developed into normal tadpoles – these were the world's first cloned animals, genetically identical to the frog

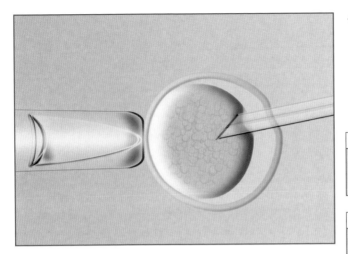

◀ Cloning begins with replacement of the genetic material in an ovum.

1952_

Briggs and King clone tadpoles, the first cloned animals

1950_

Briggs and King transplant animal cell nuclei

embryo that donated the original nucleus. Eight years later, another batch of tadpoles created by this method developed into normal frogs, the first successful cloned 'birth'.

Dolly the sheep was born on 5 July 1996, becoming the first mammal to be cloned from an adult cell. The work was carried out by a team led by Ian Wilmut at Scotland's Roslin Institute. Wilmut and his colleagues had already created clones from embryonic cells.

## ⊳ SIGHTINGS IN SCI-FI

- There was an early description of something close to cloning in Aldous Huxley's *Brave New World* (1932), with humans being grown in a hatchery.

- The first major novel to focus on human cloning was A E Van Vogt's 1945 *The World of Null-A*, while in 1968 Ursula Le Guin published a story, *Nine Lives*, about 10 clones who join the staff of a small spacecraft, nine of whom die in a mining accident.

- The idea of cloning was popular in the 1970s, as Cold War propaganda on both sides led authors to question their own freedom of thought. Clones featured in novels such as Richard Cowper's *Clone* (1972), Nancy Freedman's *Joshua, Son of None* (1973), Joe Haldeman's *The Forever War* (1974), and Ben Bova's *The Multiple Man* (1976).

- More recently, Booker Prize-winner Kazuo Ishiguro's novel *Never Let Me Go* (2005) and Michel Houellebecq's *The Possibility of an Island* (2006) explore the moral consequences of cloning human beings.

◀ Identical twins are naturally occuring clones – siblings that are born genetically identical to one another.

**1960_**

Cloned tadpoles develop into frogs for the first time

**1996_**

Dolly the sheep, the first mammal cloned from an adult cell

**2005_**

The first cloned dog, Snuppy, is created

## ⸬ REALITY

⸬ After the birth of the first cloned mammal, Dolly the sheep, in 1996, thoughts naturally turned to human cloning. In 2004, many believed it had happened for the first time: in two papers in the journal *Science*, Dr Woo Suk Hwang of Seoul National University in South Korea claimed that he and colleagues had successfully cloned a human blastocyst (the hollow ball of cells formed some four or five days after the egg is fertilized). He also claimed the team had derived embryonic stem cells from the blastocyst. However, many people were sceptical of the results and a committee at Seoul National University declared that both papers were fraudulent in early 2006, although they did accept that Dr Hwang had created the world's first cloned dog, Snuppy, in 2005.

Human cloning remains controversial and there have been movements around the world by lobby groups, governments and the United Nations to adopt a total ban on research in this area. However, some people see a difference between cloning for therapeutic purposes – such as creating stem cells that may or may not cure human disease – and reproductive cloning – the creation of an exact human clone, in the same manner as Dolly the sheep. Some countries have banned one or both, although scientists around the world continue their research in both areas.

A clone, of course, will not be identical to the original in every way – the sum of experiences and memories that makes up the human 'self' cannot be cloned, and the technology to transplant this data from an old or dying body into a healthy clone lies in the very distant future.

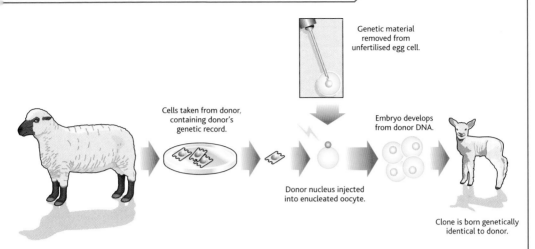

Genetic material removed from unfertilised egg cell.

Cells taken from donor, containing donor's genetic record.

Embryo develops from donor DNA.

Donor nucleus injected into enucleated oocyte.

Clone is born genetically identical to donor.

Most cloning to date, including that of Dolly the sheep and Snuppy the dog, involves a process known as somatic cell nuclear transfer:

- An unfertilised egg cell, known as an oocyte, is isolated.

- The oocyte is held by suction on the end of a thin glass tube known as a micropipette. The egg cells of most mammals typically measure about 0.1–0.2 millimetres (0.004–0.006 inches), so this needs to be done under a microscope.

- The nucleus of the egg cell, which contains the egg donor's DNA, is then removed by pricking the egg cell with a hollow glass needle and sucking it out.

- The egg cell, which is now 'enucleated', is put aside in a safe place.

- Another glass needle is inserted into a somatic cell, which is any cell other than a reproductive cell such as a sperm or egg cell. This causes the cell to break and the nucleus is drawn up inside the needle. (In the case of Dolly, the somatic cell was a mammary cell: Dolly's name comes from this, as a reference to the singer Dolly Parton.)

- This needle is then inserted into the enucleated oocyte and the contents of the needle injected. This means that the donor's DNA is now contained in the original egg, replacing the genetic material of the 'parent' animal.

- The damage to the oocyte wall made by the needle is then repaired.

- The oocyte is now zapped with a small pulse of electricity or exposed to a chemical concoction to induce cell division to start. This means the organism only carries the DNA of the donor, rather than combining with that of another 'parent'.

One of the key points is that the somatic cell has undergone what scientists call 'cell differentiation'. This means that it has transformed from a primitive cell, such as a stem cell, into a cell with a specialised function. The clever bit of the nuclear transfer method is that the contents of the host egg cell remaining after the nucleus has been removed, which is known as cytoplasm, somehow reprogramme the somatic cell nucleus to turn it back into a primitive cell. As a result, the oocyte, with its transplanted nucleus, now begins to develop in the same way as an ordinary oocyte. The procedure is not perfect, however, and only a small proportion of these cells go on to form viable embryos.

# MIND CONTROL ⋖

*Fed up with having to spend time arguing with someone to bring them around to your point of view? Get them to stare into your eyes for long enough or spike their drink with an appropriate drug and you might not need to waste your time. Secret mind control programmes are almost certainly being run by the world's governments, so next time someone suggests you have a drink and look into their eyes, watch out.*

## ⸢ SCIENTIFIC HISTORY

⸢ Throughout history, religious shamans have managed to induce trance-like states in others. One of the first people to look at these trances from the viewpoint of science was German physician Franz Mesmer in the late 1770s. Mesmer believed that medical ailments could be cured by magnetism, so he had his patients drink a solution containing iron and then asked them to hold magnetic objects. Eventually, he came to believe that he didn't need these other objects and that he himself was a source of so-called 'animal magnetism'. The term 'hypnosis' was coined by the Scottish doctor James Braid in the 1840s. He considered animal magnetism to be

## ⸢ SIGHTINGS IN SCI-FI

- Mind control, in the form of hypnosis, entered mainstream literature in George du Maurier's novel *Trilby* (1894).

- During the Cold War, rumours of brainwashed agents on both sides made mind control a sinister but popular theme. George Orwell's novel *1984* (1948) features government mind control by torture, and through the use of 'Newspeak', a language designed to suppress subversive thoughts.

- In his 1955 story 'Service Call', Philip K Dick described an artificially evolved organism capable of telepathic mind control.

fakery and conducted his own experiments into suggestion and focusing the attention onto an object. This led him to the first medically accepted basis for hypnotism.

The 'truth drug' sodium thiopental, better known by its trade name Sodium Pentothal, was discovered in 1936 by Ernest H Volwiler and Donalee L Tabern. This barbiturate is best known for its supposed ability to make those injected with it tell the truth, although it is more commonly used as an anaesthetic. In 1953, the CIA established a top-secret programme called MKULTRA, aimed at researching mind control and brainwashing. The techniques used included sensory deprivation and administering psychotropic drugs such as LSD and quinuclidinyl benzilate.

In the early 1970s, Richard Bandler, John Grinder and Gregory Bateson established a set of techniques for personal development, based on modelling the ways of working and thinking of three successful psychotherapists in different fields. Neuro-linguistic programming (NLP) incorporates the use of hypnotic language and the study of body language.

## ⁞ REALITY

⁞ Following 9/11, William Webster, a former director of the CIA and FBI, urged the US government to consider using truth drugs on terrorist suspects. Newspapers have reported that some members of al-Qaeda, particularly Abu Faraj al-Libbi, have been injected with truth drugs but there is nothing to confirm this conclusively.

Hypnosis and NLP are now widely used techniques for combating illness and enhancing personal development. In 2006, for example, researchers at the Free University of Brussels showed the efficacy of hypnosis in the treatment of alopecia (a form of stress-related baldness).

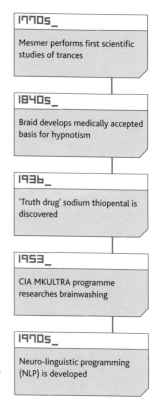

**1770s_**
Mesmer performs first scientific studies of trances

**1840s_**
Braid develops medically accepted basis for hypnotism

**1936_**
'Truth drug' sodium thiopental is discovered

**1953_**
CIA MKULTRA programme researches brainwashing

**1970s_**
Neuro-linguistic programming (NLP) is developed

## ⁞ TECH SPEC: TRUTH SERUM

- Sodium Pentothal is one of a class of chemicals known as barbiturates. These chemicals are soluble in fat and can easily cross from the blood into the brain and act upon it.

- The chemical is believed to enhance levels of the neurotransmitter gamma aminobutyric acid, causing a loss of inhibition and a greater response to suggestion.

- However, some doubt the efficacy of Sodium Pentothal as a truth serum and believe that other drugs work better – notably certain extracts of cannabis, ecstasy, LSD and alcohol.

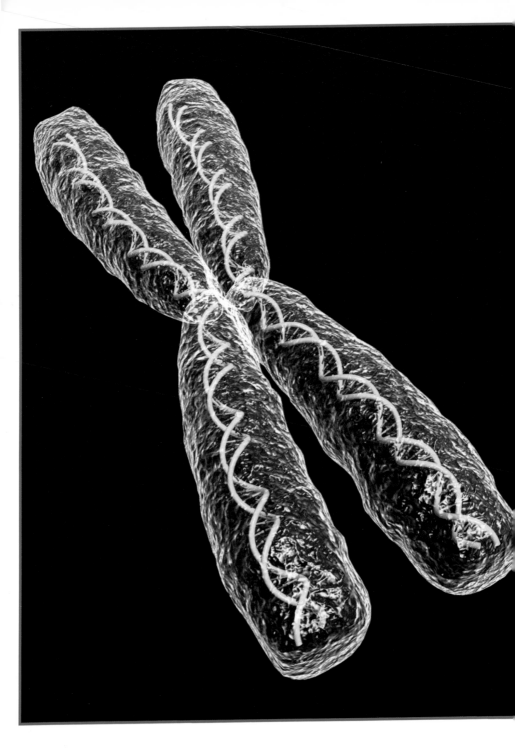

# 05:06_

# GENETIC ENGINEERING ∵

*What if we could tinker with the human genome so that all humans were immune to genetic disease, and crops were guaranteed to provide a high yield whatever the weather? As scientists tinker with genetics, we consider a future where strawberry plants yield fruit all year round and where inherited diseases are a thing of the past.*

## SCIENTIFIC HISTORY

In the 1840s, Augustinian monk Gregor Mendel carried out experiments into crossing different varieties of pea plant. His work led him to formulate three laws on how various traits, such as the height of the plants, the appearance of the seeds or the colour of the unripe pods, were passed from generation to generation.

◀ The chromosome is the vehicle by which DNA is carried and inherited.

In 1869, Swiss biologist Friedrich Miescher at the University of Tübingen isolated a number of chemicals rich in phosphates from white blood cells, known as nucleic acids, of which deoxyribonucleic

## SIGHTINGS IN SCI-FI

- In the 'Sixth Finger' episode of the television show *The Outer Limits* (1963), a man is scientifically evolved to become almost god-like.

- In Jim Smith's 1995 novel *Armed Memory*, 'microdes' are scientifically designed viruses that pass on desired traits through infection.

- In *Star Trek*, Kirk twice has to fight the genetically superior Khan (first in the television show then in the second film of the franchise).

- In *The X-Men* comics and movies and the TV show *Heroes*, genetic mutation gives rise to humans with super powers.

- In the *Resident Evil* video games and films, genetic engineering creates flesh-eating mutant zombies that threaten human survival.

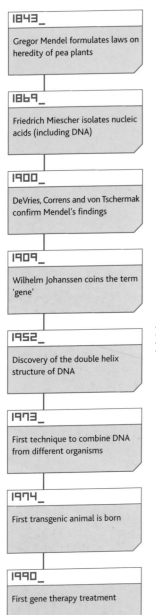

**1843_**
Gregor Mendel formulates laws on heredity of pea plants

**1869_**
Friedrich Miescher isolates nucleic acids (including DNA)

**1900_**
DeVries, Correns and von Tschermak confirm Mendel's findings

**1909_**
Wilhelm Johanssen coins the term 'gene'

**1952_**
Discovery of the double helix structure of DNA

**1973_**
First technique to combine DNA from different organisms

**1974_**
First transgenic animal is born

**1990_**
First gene therapy treatment

acid (DNA) was one. The significance of his discovery was not immediately clear. The importance of Gregor Mendel's work became clear in 1900, when three botanists, Hugo DeVries, Carl Correns and Erich von Tschermak, independently studied heredity. It was only when they looked back at previous work in the area that they rediscovered Mendel's experiments. Shortly afterwards, Danish botanist Wilhelm Johanssen coined the term 'gene'.

In 1952, work by Francis Crick, James Watson, Maurice Wilkins and Rosalind Franklin led to the discovery of the double helix structure of DNA. The technique of combining DNA from different organisms was elaborated by Herbert Boyer of the University of California at San Francisco and Stanley Cohen at Stanford University in 1973. The following year, the first transgenic animal – a mouse – was born.

Gene therapy in humans began in 1990 when Dr W French Anderson took white blood cells from a four-year-old girl suffering from a genetic problem called ADA deficiency, engineered them and reinfused them into the girl's bloodstream. However, the effect was only temporary and infusions had to be given on a regular basis.

## REALITY

Despite concerns about their long-term safety and highly vocal resistance to their use, the use of genetically modified crops has increased dramatically and millions of acres of land have been planted with them around the world. In 2004, a pig was created that had high levels of omega-3 fatty acids – one of the goals was to create a healthier pork sausage. In 2006, a company called Ventria Bioscience announced a new form of rice that had been genetically modified to include two milk proteins – lactoferrin and lysozyme. The rice was intended to combat acute diarrhoea, the second most lethal infectious disease for children under five. A study into children who ate the rice showed that they were not sick for as long as other children, were more likely to make a complete recovery and less likely to have diarrhoea in the future.

The use of genetic engineering in humans is fraught with even greater challenges, both ethical and practical, than in other animals and in plants. Progress has been slow, although in March 2006 the first clinical trial of gene therapy in the treatment of muscular dystrophy began.

# TECH SPEC: RECOMBINANT DNA

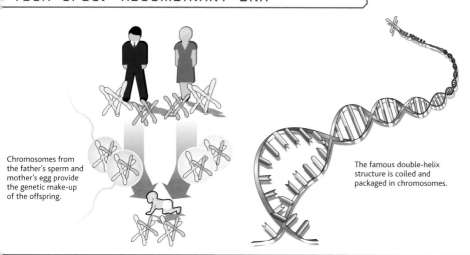

Chromosomes from the father's sperm and mother's egg provide the genetic make-up of the offspring.

The famous double-helix structure is coiled and packaged in chromosomes.

To understand how genetic engineering works, we first need to look at the building block of human life – DNA. The information contained in DNA and how it passes between parents and their offspring during reproduction is at the heart of genetics:

- DNA has a double-helix structure.

- Each helix is a long chain of nucleotides, which are molecules made up from a molecule of sugar (S), a molecule of phosphate (P) and a nitrogen-containing organic compound called a base (B).

- The bases come in only four varieties: adenine (A), cytosine (C), guanine (G) and thymine (T).

- The double-helix structure is created when these bases are bonded together with hydrogen, although adenine only bonds with thymine and cytosine with guanine.

- This complementary nature of bases enables DNA replication and the beginnings of life: if the helix is split in two, each base seeks out its complementary partner. If these bases are present in their free form, as they are in the cells of living organisms, then two copies of the original DNA are created.

- Because of the limited number of bases, the same sequences of bases frequently occur in different organisms. This is the basis of genetic engineering.

Recombinant DNA is artificially created using DNA from two distinct sources. Take wheat, for example. If we know where the DNA that confers high yield resides in cells from one kind of wheat, and where the DNA for resistance to Hessian flies lives in another, the two can be spliced together to form a hybrid. This DNA can then be used to grow a third kind of wheat, incorporating the best features of both:

- The DNA sequence that gives high yield is isolated.

- Separately, the DNA of another type of wheat that has a low yield but is resistant to attack by the Hessian fly, one of the most destructive pests facing wheat farmers, is isolated.

- Both samples of DNA are treated with so-called restriction enzymes.

- This means that the DNA can be cut at specific points in the string of bases that make up the ladder part of the helix, enabling specific sections of DNA to be 'snipped out'.

- Since the cut ends of both samples of DNA have the same sequence of bases, the snipped out DNA sequence can be inserted into the other sample.

- An enzyme called DNA ligase allows the strands to be joined back together, creating an entirely new stretch of DNA.

# 05:07_

# VIRTUAL SEX AND
# FUTURE SEX TOYS ∢

*AIDS and other sexually transmitted diseases have made 'safe sex' the buzz-phrase of
the early 21st century. And what sex could be safer than virtual sex? High-speed
computers mean that simulations can now seem more real than ever and the Internet
has opened up a world of potential virtual partners. Next will be the integration of
tactile technologies to make it all feel incredibly real.*

## ⊳ SCIENTIFIC HISTORY
⊳ Premium-rate telephone numbers appeared in the United States in
1977. These 1-900 numbers were first used for a Jimmy Carter radio
broadcast but their use for phone sex lines soon escalated.

In 1991, Howard Rheingold coined the term 'teledildonics' in his
book *Virtual Reality* to refer to sexual interaction at long-distance.
He imagined a body suit that could imitate sensations initiated by a

## ⊳ SIGHTINGS IN SCI-FI

- Barbarella's nemesis Dr Durand Durand uses 'The
Excessive Machine' on her in the 1968 movie. It is
an automated masseur that evokes multiple
orgasms, controlled using a piano-style keyboard.

- The 'orgasmatron' debuts in Woody Allen's movie
*Sleeper* (1973), in the form of a device which
causes an instant orgasm.

- In *Star Trek*, the idea that crew members could

pursue their fantasies in the holodeck led
inevitably to crew members enjoying erotic
simulations.

- In the 1993 film *Demolition Man*, a reluctant John
Spartan (Sylvester Stallone) is introduced by
Lenina Huxley (Sandra Bullock) to 'Vir-Sex' –
simulated sex without any of the mess or risks of
the real thing.

◀ Virtual reality and the Internet may soon make long-distance sexual encounters commonplace.

partner elsewhere on the planet. The advent of the Internet in the mid-1990s provided a communications structure ideal for such interaction and led to a huge increase in virtual sex. Instant, free access to partners across the globe, with no strings attached, has proved a potent combination. In particular, some users of Internet chatrooms and instant messenger applications began to share their sexual fantasies with other users. The proliferation of webcams has added a visual element to these virtual encounters.

## ⸬ REALITY

⸬ The science of haptics allows computer users to sense touch when using certain programs. Much of this development has taken place in the world of video games, where force-feedback joysticks and steering wheels vibrate in response to actions (for example, gunfire or off-road driving) on screen. It is not hard to imagine how these might be incorporated into virtual sexual encounters.

## ⸬ TECH SPEC: SINULATOR

It had to happen some time – sex toys that can be controlled over the Internet have arrived with the Sinulator dildo, a classic example of teledildonics:

- The dildo is plugged into your PC.

- The dildo is then controlled remotely by a third party through an interface that looks like the control panel from a 1980s arcade driving game.

- The system also allows sex toys to be connected together over the Internet, with faster action at one end translating into a more feverish response at the other.

- If you don't have a willing partner, there are online sex games that send signals to your device at predetermined moments.

# FUTURE CLOTHING ❖

*Fashions may come and go but one recent trend that looks set to run and run is clothing that does something more than keep you warm. How about smart clothing that incorporates environmental control systems to keep the wearer cool in summer and warm in winter? Or a second skin that automatically monitors your vital signs or even enhances your own strength?*

## ⫸ SCIENTIFIC HISTORY

⫸ Until the 20th century, everyone wore clothing made from natural materials. Since then, developments in chemistry have allowed new textiles to be created that are cheaper and stronger than anything in nature. In the 1920s, Charles Macintosh discovered a technique to make coats waterproof, while 30 years later Swiss chemist Georges Audemars came up with rayon as an artificial alternative to silk.

The firm DuPont has been an innovator in this area – nylon appeared in 1935 and ever-so-stretchy Lycra in 1959, while Kevlar, a lightweight fibre five times stronger than steel, first became available in 1971. Lightweight, waterproof, stretchy and tough –

## ⫸ SIGHTINGS IN SCI-FI

- In *When the Sleeper Wakes* (1899), H G Wells predicts a machine that instantly produces suits of clothing to an individual's measurements.

- In 1972, Larry Niven and David Gerrold describe an 'impact suit' in *The Flying Sorcerers* – a flexible suit that converts to rigid armour on impact to protect its wearer.

- In his 1977 novel *Dying of the Light*, George R R Martin invented 'chameleon cloth', which changes colour to match its surroundings. William Gibson's *Neuromancer* (1984) describes more fashion-conscious clothing that can change its design based on recorded images or real-time picture input.

these materials formed the basis of modern sports gear, military clothing and armour, and of course, high-tech space suits.

That same year, J F Annis and P Webb conceived the Space Activity Suit, the first design to use a revolutionary technology called mechanical counterpressure (MCP). This comprised seven layers of elastic material and came with a gas-filled helmet and chest bladder to provide adequate breathing pressure. Further MCP concepts appeared in the years that followed, although NASA have yet to commence full-scale work on any of the proposals.

## ⠶ REALITY

⠶ One snowboard clothing firm has created a jacket that incorporates wiring to control an MP3 player. It includes all the usual player controls on a panel located on the arm and a socket in an interior pocket for connecting the player.

Researchers at the Textile and Fibre Technology arm of the CSIRO research institute in Australia have been working on textiles that incorporate fine data-conducting polymers as part of the actual cloth. The researchers hope to be able to create a vest for athletes that doubles as a biomonitoring device and can withstand a tumble in the washing machine.

In late 2005, Professor Dave J Newman and colleagues produced a report on biosuits for astronauts for NASA's Institute for Advanced Concepts, which funds proposals for revolutionary projects for the aeronautics and space sectors. These biosuits differ radically from traditional space suits; they are more like a second skin and are kept intact under vacuum by mechanical counterpressure. Professor Newman also envisioned that this second skin would incorporate electrically actuated artificial muscle fibres to enhance human strength and stamina.

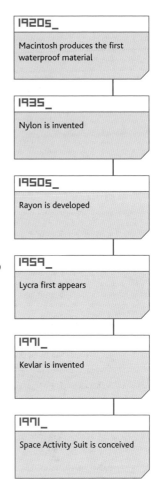

**1920s_**

Macintosh produces the first waterproof material

**1935_**

Nylon is invented

**1950s_**

Rayon is developed

**1959_**

Lycra first appears

**1971_**

Kevlar is invented

**1971_**

Space Activity Suit is conceived

## ⠶ TECH SPEC: SPACE SUITS

- Current space suits use rigid outers that are pressurised throughout with gas and cause significant problems with movement, particularly in the cramped conditions of a spacecraft.

- Mechanical counterpressure suits are made from an elastic material and exert pressure on the skin in the same way as a leotard. To ensure a tight fit and maintain good pressure on the skin, the suit must be custom-made for the wearer.

# FUTURE FOOD ⋖

*What if, in an instant, you could have any food you desired simply by pushing a button: filet mignon, medium rare, with garlic mashed potatoes; your mother's apple pie; or even fish and chips like the ones from your favourite chippy. Imagine being able to have any of those foods – or any other culinary concoction you desire – prepared perfectly, on demand. That's the promise of the food replicator.*

## ⋗ SCIENTIFIC HISTORY

⋗ Food science has provided many time-saving inventions over the years: canned foods in the 17th century, instant coffee in 1901, Clarence Birdseye's frozen meals in 1923 and Swanson's 'TV dinners' in 1954. The last few decades have also seen the emergence of labour-saving devices such as food processors and microwave ovens, allowing a revolution in on-demand food preparation. Automatic cooking technology started with coffee vending machines in 1973 and evolved to French fry vending machines by 2003. Perhaps the most advanced recipe assembly machine is the bread maker (first introduced in 1986 in Japan), which can combine multiple ingredients with multiple processing steps to bake a loaf of bread with minimal human input.

1923_

First frozen food available in shops

Today, NASA is working on a food replicator that could be used in space. The fridge-sized device could process dozens of ingredients into hundreds and perhaps thousands of recipes to produce a massive menu of meals. Of course, this machine would have to be self-cleaning and easy to replenish with myriad basic ingredients. The dream, however, is to build food molecule by molecule. While that is not yet possible, rapid prototyping machines use a technique called stereo lithography to 'print' 3D parts and moulds out of plastic, in a similar way to inkjet printers, which precisely spray

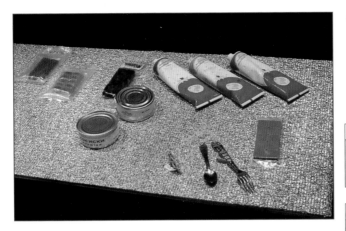

◀ Dehydrated food has been a staple for astronauts since the 1960s.

1970s_

Microwave ovens first mass-produced

1970s_

Cuisinart food processer is unveiled

1954_

First 'TV dinners' appear

microdroplets to print a photo. Scientists are also experimenting with ways to 'print' biological material to create a steak, sparing the cell-donor cow.

## ⫸ REALITY

⫸ The NASA food synthesiser is more of a compact cooking machine than a *Star Trek* replicator. However, it would be capable of creating hundreds of dishes from raw materials, keeping astronauts happy and full during extended space travel. Such a device could be adapted for Earth cuisine, perhaps in school cafeterias, on aeroplanes or even at home.

To replicate food *Star Trek*-style would require a computer able to record the exact molecular makeup of a given dish, a store of

## ⫸ SIGHTINGS IN SCI-FI

- The food synthesiser first appeared with the publication of John Campbell's story 'Twilight' in the magazine *Astounding Science Fiction* in 1934.

- Years later, in the 1960s, we saw the Jetsons' food synthesiser generate any meal in its database.

- However, nowhere has the food synthesiser fantasy been better illustrated than in several generations of the *Star Trek* shows and movies.

Replication evolved as the starships did – in one early 1960s episode, children choose from cards, each containing data for different flavours of ice cream. By the time we reach *The Next Generation* (1987–1994), Captain Picard simply has to ask for 'Earl Grey, hot', and it is created through voice-recognition from information in the computer's memory banks.

◄ Meals in dehydrated or pill form may be technologically possible, but would be anything but appetising.

1973_

First automatic coffee vending machine

1986_

Automatic bread maker is introduced in Japan

atoms from the various elements that make it up, and the ability to reassemble those atoms into the exact molecular structure of the foodstuff. Moreover, for the food to have the correct texture, rather than appearing as mush, these molecules would then have to be assembled to form the cells and fibres that make up a steak or a carrot. Given that just $1/3$ ounce (10 grams) of carbon contains $6 \times 10^{23}$ atoms, producing a quarter-pounder this way will require significant technological advances.

## ⟩ TECH SPEC: NASA POLYMENU

NASA's polymenu cooking device would assemble meals in a step-by-step fashion similar to the way a paint-by-numbers artist could re-create the Mona Lisa. Recipes would first have to be reconstituted into a formula that the machine can follow. This science is called 'molecular gastronomy', a term popularised by French scientist Hervé This. For example, to create puff pastry you would follow this process:

- Puff pastry is obtained by putting a layer of butter (B) in an envelope made of dough (D).

- The dough is then stretched and folded into three, which can be defined as DBD.

- This stretching and folding is repeated six times, defined as (DBD)(DBD)(DBD)or D(BD)3, which is two layers of dough (D) that come in contact to make one.

- The second folding of the six repetitions produces D(BD)9, and subsequently D(BD)27, D(BD)81, D(BD)243 and finally D(BD)729.

Dr This further defines dough as 'a dispersion of starch granules (S1) in a gluten network (S2)'. He gives butter the formula (W/O)/S. So, the final formula of puff pastry, ignoring the proportions of ingredients, is: (S1/S2)(((W/O)/S)(S1/S2)729).

Using this symbolic language, it should be possible to create millions of new and exciting meals using a high-tech food processor with minimal physical labour. NASA scientists envision the food-assembly machine as a series of processing chambers and holding vats that would work as an automated production line. The chambers and vats would be attached by pipes and could heat or cool ingredients. Each chamber would be assigned a specific purpose – whipping, sautéeing, mixing, baking, cooling, and so on. The machine would be stocked with a series of long-life ingredients that would have multiple uses in thousands, and perhaps millions, of recipes.

# CRYONICS ⫶

*You don't have to give up on life when the doctor hands you a terminal diagnosis or even signs your death certificate. Instead, you can choose to chill out in cold storage until medical science figures out how to cure and reanimate you in the future. The same technique could one day be used to allow astronauts to survive deep space travel, or even to give people the option to bail out of their current life so they can live in a better tomorrow.*

## ⫶ SCIENTIFIC HISTORY

The first steps in the development of cryonics were taken in the 1960s, when Robert Ettinger and Evan Cooper (writing as Nathan Duhring) theorised that freezing the newly dead could preserve their bodies until such a time that the technology existed to revive them. Since then, numerous for-profit and non-profit cryonics service organisations have come and gone, of which the only notable survivors are Alcor in Arizona and the Cryonics Institute in Michigan.

In the 1980s, Mike Darwin, co-founder of the Institute for Advanced Biological studies (IABS), worked with Jerry Leaf, medical researcher at the University of California, Los Angeles (UCLA), to provide the cryonics field with better preservation techniques. These included CPR and cardiopulmonary bypasses to keep blood circulating through the body, delivering nutrients and oxygen.

To date, the most famous subscriber to cryonics is baseball great Ted Williams, whose head was cryopreserved by Alcor in 2002. Urban myth has it that Walt Disney was cryopreserved but this is exactly that – a myth.

## ⫶ THE REALITY

Although the freezing process appears to have been mastered, medical science does not yet have the technology to repair the

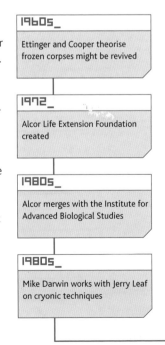

**1960s_**

Ettinger and Cooper theorise frozen corpses might be revived

**1972_**

Alcor Life Extension Foundation created

**1980s_**

Alcor merges with the Institute for Advanced Biological Studies

**1980s_**

Mike Darwin works with Jerry Leaf on cryonic techniques

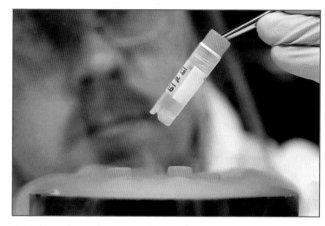
▲ DNA samples can be preserved at very low temperatures.

**2006_**

US doctors put pigs in stasis and revive them with no ill effects

**2005_**

Alcor starts to use vitrification to store bodies

**2005_**

Safar Center revives dogs that had been dead for three hours

**1986_**

Drexler suggests repairing dead cells using nanotechnology

damage and revive you, so you may end up in cold statis for a century or two, if not longer. A nano-repair process would be needed before resuscitation to fix tissue damage at the molecular level and undo the damage caused by disease, ageing or the cause of death. This has yet to be invented, although Alcor's customers remain hopeful.

## ⸰ SIGHTINGS IN SCI-FI

- Originally introduced as 'cold sleep' in Robert Heinlein's 1941 novel *Methuselah's Children*, the idea of freezing yourself for the future has become a staple in sci-fi. However, it was the 1997 cult novel *The First Immortal*, which explores the science and philosophy of cryonics, that has convinced a growing number of people that the deep freeze is a viable option for our lifetime.

- The idea of freezing yourself is especially popular where space travel is concerned – for example, in the *Aliens* series, the main character Ripley and her fellow space travellers are put into cold sleep during their long journeys. Another common theme is the idea of waking up to a dramatically altered future after a period in cold stasis: in the 1973 comedy *Sleeper*, Woody Allen wakes up in a Fascist future; and in the television series *Futurama*, Philip Fry is accidentally frozen in stasis on New Year's Eve 2000 and revived into a futuristic world a thousand years later.

- The moral issues surrounding cryonics are also explored in fiction. In his 1986 novel *Fiasco*, Stanislaw Lem asked whether a person who revives with amnesia is still the same person who was initially frozen. More recently, in *Vanilla Sky* (the 2001 remake of the 1997 Spanish film *Open Your Eyes*) Tom Cruise's character must ultimately choose whether to continue in a 'lucid dream' created by cryonics company Life Extension, or to re-enter the real world.

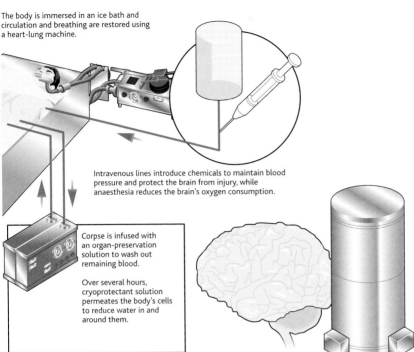

The body is immersed in an ice bath and circulation and breathing are restored using a heart-lung machine.

Intravenous lines introduce chemicals to maintain blood pressure and protect the brain from injury, while anaesthesia reduces the brain's oxygen consumption.

Corpse is infused with an organ-preservation solution to wash out remaining blood.

Over several hours, cryoprotectant solution permeates the body's cells to reduce water in and around them.

Body is cooled with nitrogen gas to -124°C over a period of three hours.

Over the next three weeks, it is further cooled to -196°C and stored long-term in a tank of liquid nitrogen.

- Alcor, the world's largest cryonics company, believes that a person's memory and personality are preserved in the brain after legal death and that there is therefore a window of opportunity in which the brain's structure can be preserved.

- The patient, as Alcor calls a client, is immersed in an ice bath, and circulation and breathing are restored using a heart-lung machine. Intravenous lines introduce chemicals into the body to maintain blood pressure and protect the brain from injury, while anaesthesia is used to reduce the brain's oxygen consumption and prevent tissue breakdown.

- The heart-lung machine cools the body to just above the freezing point of water and the patient's blood is replaced with an organ preservation solution.

- The patient is infused with a preservation solution. Over several hours, this cryoprotectant begins to permeate the body's cells, the goal being to reduce water in and around the cells – as water freezes, it creates crystals that destroy cell structures.

- In this process, the brain vitrifies (and the body partially vitrifies and partially freezes) into a glass-like state. The patient is then cooled with nitrogen gas to −124°C (−191°F) over a period of three hours. Over the next three weeks, they are further cooled to −196°C (−320°F) and stored long-term in a tank, called a dewar, which contains liquid nitrogen.

# INDEX ⁖

# INDEX